A Master Alignment® Book

The
Power of Love

*The Key to Opening the
Gifts Hidden in Our DNA*

Michelle Andersen

Master Alignment is a Registered Trademark

Portions of this book previously appeared in a different form in Moving Into Master Alignment, published in 1997. That book is now out of print.

Kathleen Hill, Editor
Ferdinand Mels, Cover Design www.spiritfractal.com
Suzanne Waterman, Book Design and Layout

PRINTED IN THE UNITED STATES OF AMERICA

ISBN 0-91713805-0-3

Dedicated to

All my Teachers...
especially those who call themselves
my students.

In Appreciation

❖ To all those who over the years have wittingly or unwittingly helped to nurture Master Alignment's growth by receiving a personal session or attending our programs. This is especially true for all Practitioners and Awakeners who have contributed so much despite having such full professional and personal lives.

❖ To the pioneers like Practitioners Charlotte and Melissa Abell, Regina Stuckey, Christina Ludy, and Mary Lou Beatman who—airline ticket in hand—brought this work into so many new locations presenting workshops and facilitating hundreds of personal sessions. Because of their efforts, this work was introduced not only into new areas of this country, but also in Canada, Norway, Switzerland, Germany, and Australia.

For work on this book:

❖ To all whose Transmissions contributed towards building the body of knowledge.

❖ To Canadian Practitioner and graphics artist Ferdinand Mels, for the magnificent cover artwork.

❖ To Practitioner Kathy Hill, a professional editor who provided the kindest and most thorough editing any writer could want. If there are any mistakes in this book, they are mine alone.

❖ To Awakener Susan Fenley who offered assistance proofreading portions of the manuscript.

❖ To Awakener Patricia Stout and her husband Jon who helped to make our dream a reality.

❖ To Practitioners Jason Pirro, Laura Jenkins and Mary Beth Sullivan, for your friendship, love and support—there simply are no words!

❖ Finally, yet never last, to my partner Richard Rylander: This book could only have been done because of all that you are.

My Gratitude, Love, and Blessings—M.A.

Contents

Introduction

*H*ave you ever watched a movie that had a surprise ending—a twist that gave an entirely new meaning to the plot and made you want to see it again? Why again? Because you wanted to view the story through new eyes and at another, higher level of awareness.

That is the goal of this book: to give you the power to see yourself and your life in a new, more loving and expanded way.

The twist? We call this "the missing piece." It is based on new information that has answered hundreds of previously unanswerable questions.

At one level, Master Alignment offers unique insights into the relationship between the mind, the emotions, and the body. At a higher level, this new understanding, along with the processes based on it, is designed to promote humanity's growth in consciousness. We do this first by exploring the unique role our bodies—and specifically our DNA—have played not only in human development, but in our individual lives.

This is not a scientific treatise, far from it. Neither is it exclusively a metaphysical work. From our perspective, Master Alignment touches many areas of life, as reflected by the clients we have worked with over the years: They are physicians, psychotherapists, artists, educators, researchers, physical therapists, accountants, government employees, and engineers, as well as entrepreneurs, athletes, computer programmers, metaphysical practitioners, and countless others.

The emerging field of Psychogenetics will likely be responsible for *scientifically* documenting the DNA's expanded role in our lives. However, our knowledge comes in another way: using higher faculties of mind—the intuition—on behalf of individuals who can find no solutions to certain problems or blocks. Our "testing laboratory" is the home, the workplace, and the playing field. Our "standards": Does it explain the unexplainable in a way that is both verifiable and without judgment? Does it significantly change lives, and for the better?

Beginning in 1989, the new information appeared in response to the question of why, despite all their efforts, certain otherwise successful women could not find a committed relationship. They did not want to be passively "owned" by or dependent on men; they wanted the seeming impossible—to find an equal partner.

The initial answer was that the women were experiencing vague fears around being alone, and this was creating their reality. More importantly, we learned, beneath this fear they also carried an ancient belief that without a man, a woman could not survive. Although still the prevailing reality in some third-world countries, this belief had no validity in their lives today.

We then were told that this fear around not having a man to support them was not in the brain, *it was imprinted in the DNA* and thus was passed on generation after generation. Being in the body, this outdated fear was impervious to change by the usual methods. A new technique, which we describe in this book, had to be used to clear this level of imprinting.

Since 1989 we have uncovered and cleared hundreds of other outdated issues for thousands of men and women. This book, modeled on the Master Alignment Program *Transforming the DNA*, can only include a portion of these. Yet we believe there are enough so that all readers will find at least one "surprising twist" that offers them expanded understanding and, perhaps, a new set of eyes with which to view their personal life story.

Part One:
"It's In the Body"

"It's in the Body!"

*T*hroughout time, many cultures recorded their history not in stone or on scrolls but in an unwritten form. They used story, poetry, song, and dance to immortalize both historical events and important teachings. Today we receive the latest information through newspapers, books, magazines, and the Internet. In addition, we continue the oral tradition by communicating through radio, television, lectures, workshops, movies, plays, and even by telephone. Yet the oldest and most comprehensive source of recorded human information may not be any of these forms—it may actually be our own bodies.

It is a truth being verified by modern science more each day: While we may *think* that we store information only in our minds, the human body in fact has another "mind of its own." This "other mind" is in the body within the DNA located at the center of every cell.

Human DNA is comprised of two parts: 1 percent, or 300,000 units, is genetic information—that portion which was recently mapped by the Human Genome Project. The remaining 99 percent, or *2.9 billion units*, is currently labeled "Junk DNA" by Science, which does not know or understand its purpose.

Since 1989, we have been demonstrating that the 99 percent portion of nongenetic DNA contains vast amounts of intelligent information, gathered from our ancestors' and our own past experiences. We call this portion of the DNA the **BodyMind.**

The data in the body's library is recorded to support humanity's overall evolutionary development as well as to promote physical survival. If the body had not adopted such a permanent system of recording information in the DNA to be passed down through the ages, it would have been necessary for humans to "begin at the beginning" every time a child was born. There would never have been a Mozart, or an Einstein, for example. More importantly, we would have had to relearn all the basic information that supports self-preservation.

Just as all animals are born with instinctual knowledge designed to ensure their survival, information stored in the BodyMind is meant to preserve the species by promoting survival of the physical body. In its capacity as protector of the human species, the BodyMind also contains a built-in alarm system—a triggering apparatus designed to warn us, through our emotions, when the human body is in danger. The BodyMind's primary tool for this purpose is the emotion of fear. As the animals show us by their example, the true purpose of fear is to alert us when our bodies may be in danger.

While much of the imprinted DNA information is both valid and useful today, some of its "survival triggers" may be outdated—and creating unnecessary problems in our lives. We may recall an experience when, for no apparent reason, we somehow either could not do something that we wanted to do, or we could not help doing something, even though it made no logical sense. Similarly, we may recall a long-held desire that we had given up hope of ever achieving, because somehow we felt inexplicably blocked. These are examples of the BodyMind overruling the logical mind, while applying itself to ensuring the body's survival.

In our new understanding of the effect of outdated information in the DNA, it becomes possible to identify and actually clear blocks still held in the BodyMind, thus freeing us to go forward unfettered by old, fear-based beliefs.

Emotions and the BodyMind

If it were true that "everything begins in the mind"—that emotions are always reactions to thoughts initiated by the brain—it would seem that we could stop painful emotions by simply changing our thoughts. This can become confusing when we recognize that there are many times we feel anger, fear, or emotional pain without knowing what thoughts—or even what events—triggered our feelings. When we cannot find a *rational* reason for our emotional reactions, we are told it is because they are caused by our subconscious thoughts. Today this understanding serves as a basis for most systems of modern psychotherapy, especially those seeking to uncover the subconscious processes that lead to unwanted emotions or inappropriate actions.

While subconscious thoughts may indeed trigger our emotions in many instances, that explanation is still somehow incomplete. Therapists, especially, find themselves working for months, if not years, using their best techniques with patients, without being able to break through to eradicate some core issues. Yet an answer seems closer if we apply the understanding that there is another mind—the BodyMind—which can trigger powerful emotional reactions even faster than the thoughts of the rational mind; and further, that the BodyMind is vastly more comprehensive than the brain, because it contains information that is tens of thousands of years old.

We agree with those therapies which hold that there is a need to find our hidden "belief and emotional complexes," followed by the necessity of making new choices to unravel or release them. We differ, however, on the *location* of some of those hidden complexes—which we call **Patterns.** Saying, "It's in the body!" helps us release the limiting idea that every emotional problem can be solved by the mere act of discovering and changing subconscious thoughts in the brain. If, as we assert, a number of our blocking Patterns are located in the DNA—as beliefs that are part of the survival information imprinted and stored in the BodyMind—no amount of rational reprogramming will be effective in changing them, or their effect on our lives.

Science itself seems to be growing more aware of the impact of DNA on the emotions. In 1998, Candace Pert, Ph.D. a neuroscientist and research professor at Georgetown University Medical Center, wrote a book titled *Molecules of Emotion,* discussing the effects of neuropeptides on the creation of emotional states in the body. The book—considered groundbreaking— offers an assertion to the effect that neuropeptides' chemical reactions are programmed by information in the DNA; yet, this idea is never explored further.

If we are to uncover the reasons for our fear-based actions and emotions, we must examine the information in the DNA, focusing especially on the blocking Patterns. Throughout this book, we will explore this subject through story, myths, and archetypes in the way our ancestors learned. Not only have we found this an effective way to teach, it is the manner in which most of this information was imparted to us. The stories in this book are from written intuitive readings or **Transmissions** that were received in a conscious, whole-brained state. They are merely representative of the thousands of other sessions that were taped for clients and never copied or transcribed.

These stories do not belong to one person; they belong to all of us: The hard lessons and the easy ones, the triumphs that overcome the fears, the talents that grow out of the pain, and most especially, the wealth of wisdom in all of it.

Defining Patterns

We have briefly described a Pattern as a complex combination of unconscious beliefs derived from past survival experiences that manifest today as pain, fear, or blocks in our life. All Patterns have certain characteristics in common. Knowing these will help us recognize them.

Repetition is one of the major characteristics of all Patterns. The very word "Pattern" connotes something that has a repeated design: a white sheet is plain, while one with a floral print is clearly patterned. If we have a hidden fear that is blocking us, we have already experienced it many different times and in diverse ways. An isolated instance of trauma or pain is not necessarily a Pattern; it might simply be a new learning experience. Once we can name the fear, it is easier for us to recognize past instances of it in our lives.

Patterns are complex because they can contain a major belief—such as "I am unworthy"—and several minor beliefs based upon it: "Those I love will abandon me (because I am unworthy)." "I will not get promoted (because I am unworthy)." "People won't talk to me at the party (because I am unworthy)." "I work harder than everyone else (because I am unworthy)." Even in this simple example, the potential list of beliefs is endless.

All fear Patterns generate emotions such as shame, discouragement, grief, rage, fear, sorrow—another endless list. Generally, the emotion will arise when an event, thought, or memory triggers the Pattern belief. The smallest thing may cause an instantaneous emotional chain reaction, giving rise to a response that is out of proportion to the circumstances. If we were to have a Pattern around feeling unworthy and were called into the boss's office, for example, we might incorrectly presume that the boss intends to discuss our failures (and thus validate our unworthiness). Because all Patterns have an underlying basis in survival, this might then engender thoughts of being fired and subsequently losing our friends, car and home—before we have even entered the office.

There are also times when a Pattern's emotional component is triggered outside our conscious awareness; we suddenly feel pain or fear without knowing why. A stranger arches an eyebrow—we feel devastated and ashamed. Although we have no way of knowing what that person is thinking, our body may be "reliving" an ancient humiliation. The body's survival mechanism is so sensitive that its immediate reactions are faster than the mind can reason. Although we feel shame in the present moment, we do so without understanding that the real humiliation was experienced and imprinted in the far-distant past.

All Patterns are holographic in nature; by "touching in" on any fragment of a Pattern we will also make an instantaneous yet unconscious connection not only to the underlying core belief, but also to the life-and-death fear connected to it. The fear of speaking in public is fairly common. If we have past imprinting from being tortured for expressing our personal beliefs, we might presently be unable to render a simple opinion on any subject, for fear that others will persecute us.

Remember that fear is always a warning about the potential for danger to the physical body. On the surface, it might not appear survival is at stake when we are called into the boss's office. If we tend to avoid criticism or have issues around authority, our *body* may have sufficient reason, based on its past recorded history, to believe we are being summoned to our eventual death. Our physical and emotional reactions give us a clue of just how serious the underlying belief is to our body—even if it is no longer valid.

These examples demonstrate another characteristic of all Patterns: they operate outside normal time; hence, they rarely give us correct information about our present circumstances. Unlike the brain, the BodyMind has no sense of what time—or what century—it is. To its way of thinking, all its Patterned "truths" are as valid today as they were the moment they were imprinted. This works well when the BodyMind reminds us not to put our hand in a fire, but not when it insists that an *outdated*, fear-based belief must be honored for its validity. A fear of crossing the street unescorted is healthy in a three-year-old: however, this same fear is pathological in an otherwise healthy thirty-year-old.

Finally, Patterns unconsciously control our choices. We might compare the BodyMind to a computer, while Patterns are the "programs" in the hard drive. Patterns imprinted into the DNA are programmed to open and run automatically under certain specific conditions. We have long forgotten about them—if we even knew of them at all—and hence are not even aware they are still operating today. If we try to do something that is counter to the instructions written into the Pattern, our body will insistently send us an "error message," sometimes using an intense emotion, and at others a physical reaction. If we become inured to this "alarm" we might find we are still prevented from going forward. Inertia, distractions, even what is termed "self-sabotage" are only a few ways that we unknowingly honor our Pattern's prohibitions.

Quantity of Patterns

Even if we were to limit our definition of the word Pattern to those that evoke some form of fear, we are all still likely to hold thousands of Patterns in our DNA; not all of these may be actively running, however. Everything in the human condition, if taken to an extreme, can lead to its becoming a Pattern. Because we have a vast informational inheritance from our ancestors, we can also presume we carry an enormous variety of fear Patterns with different degrees of intensity.

The Soul determines which Patterns will be recessive and which active. We might use a shopping metaphor to describe how, out of an infinite number of possibilities, the Soul chooses the particular qualities, characteristics, gifts, challenges—and Patterns—that will be dominant in each individual's life.

While families may "inherit" Patterns, each individual family member still has their own unique combination not duplicated in the others. For example, one descendant of refugees may exhibit a lifelong, pervasive fear of loss, while a sibling with the same ancestry might have only a few issues around lack, yet may never feel secure or at home regardless of where they live or how long they have been there.

Depending on its intensity, a single event can generate multiple fear Patterns. One highly intuitive client journaled her session. After recording the story, she was inspired to list not only the fear Patterns discussed, but those her intuitive guidance offered in addition. Through this woman's story, we see just how intricate, far-reaching, and interconnected fear Patterns from one tragic experience can be. What follows is an excerpt from her journal, beginning with the story—or personal myth—and ending with some inspirational words from her Guides.

"The Disowned Daughter"

In the Middle Ages, the young daughter of a wealthy man falls in love with the horse trainer, to the great consternation of her father, who sends her off to the convent. Sometime before she departs, the lovers meet one last time. As a result of that assignation the young woman becomes pregnant, a fact she discovers later in the nunnery. When her condition becomes clear, the Mother Superior sends her home to her father in disgrace. He turns her away at the door and, upon learning the truth, has the horse trainer killed.

With no home, money, or reputation she wanders alone in the forest, surviving as a gypsy or beggar would, disowned, disgraced, despairing, and grief-stricken. She goes into labor prematurely and dies alone on the forest floor, her baby dying as well.

These are the fear beliefs created by this experience:
- having a nearly complete distrust of self;
- taking responsibility for the feelings and welfare of loved ones far beyond the realm of reality;
- being willing to endure all manner of suffering to ensure the welfare of those she holds dear;
- being unable to defend herself against attacks on her personage and dignity;
- having an intense fear of being discovered;
- looking in vain for "home";
- fearing being thrown out of any place of rest for sins she may commit unknowingly;
- feeling her best is never going to be good enough;
- feeling that love kills;
- believing it is unsafe and unwise to love intensely;

- feeling overly protective toward those she does love;
- fearing the effects of her actions on those she loves out of proportion to their power to harm;
- feeling powerless to stop those she loves from being harmed or killed;
- finding herself inarticulate in her own defense; and
- feeling that she always needs to be ready to move on when there is any sign of disapproval before anyone has a chance to be harsh.

Thus, a kind of homeless or vagabond personality was created, one feeling unworthy of love and home; daring not to want or try to have love and home; feeling hunted, haunted and on the run; feeling her very presence creates danger for those she loves. There is also the aspect of physical expression of great and encompassing love. To love is not a crime. To become pregnant in the act of loving is not a crime and yet, in that society, in those days, both were treated as worthy of death; hence creating the additional Patterns of:

- deep distrust of the body;
- deep distrust of the emotions;
- feeling ashamed;
- fear of sex; and
- an inability to be comfortable with passion.

All this may be removed as you process this information. In its place will be only intense Spiritual Light, the Creative Light of the Divine Universe. Fear it not, for it is the stuff of power and peace. It cannot harm, it can only bring good. And though you know not what form that good will take, be assured it will take form, as a new day cannot be predicted from a night, yet just as surely will it come. Rest, child, in complete comfort and peace. You are always in our most tender care.

In carefully reading this story, it appears that all her difficulties began when she fell in love with the horse trainer. This led to her undoing—to pregnancy, rejection, shame, and, ultimately, her death and those of her lover and child. The holographically encoded message in her DNA was clear—"Love leads to death." Even her Guides pointed this out in their litany of her Patterns. There is no question that, to her BodyMind, Love was the cause of her tragedy. Yet, the real irony is this is true of all Patterns: they all begin with Love—as that concept is defined by each person at a particular Soul age.

In this situation, her father was "in love" with his reputation and, very likely, with his own goals for his daughter's future. If he determined that it was socially abhorrent—and therefore damaging to him—for his daughter to have a relationship with a hired hand, to his mind he was attempting to "save" her, while also protecting his own image. By rejecting her after she was cast out of the convent, he may have been acting as a very young Soul, whose values place one's social standing as above personal relationships. It is also the younger Souls who see their children as "assets." In that time, a father often made a business or power alliance by marrying his daughter to another family of his own choosing. By becoming involved with the trainer, the daughter threatened his wealth and power—especially when she had obviously defied him. The father would have seen this as a form of "theft." That explanation does not *excuse* his behavior—or that of the daughter, the Mother Superior, or the horse trainer. This was a painful experience for each of them, and one that held a wealth of learning, which is the real purpose behind all experience. Continuing to focus on what happened "to her" would keep the client's wisdom hidden, thus requiring still *another* painful experience, until the wisdom was finally integrated.

Every Pattern "story" is a Love story, no matter how horrifying the facts or events portrayed. This is true when we are the perpetrators and when we are the victims. Remember that the opposite of Love is not hate, it is indifference. If seen through the "eyes of Love" much that we or others might judge to be negative is perhaps our best attempt to survive in the world. That is why it is impossible to judge without knowing the whole truth within any situation.

The only reason we can experience fear is because we love. Wanting to preserve and protect our body is a form of self-preservation, therefore it is also self–love. We fear harming those close to us or having them harmed by others because we love them. There is no fear that is not directly related to Love. This also applies to all that we do, think, imagine, or believe. If closely scrutinized—and despite all judgments to the contrary—each will have some basis in Love.

Because they are created out of Love, the fact that we have Patterns is never judged. There is nothing "wrong" with having Patterns, unless we also see self-preservation or love of others as "wrong." What is important is releasing the fear that overshadows the Love and wisdom at their heart.

Conditioned Patterns

*P*atterns are formed through trauma, conditioning, and vows—and each of these will be illustrated many times throughout this book. "The Disowned Daughter" Transmission is merely one example of a Pattern created by a traumatic event.

Because Patterns are highly subjective, the individual body determines what is life-threatening and what must be recorded in the DNA as such, regardless of how someone else might judge the same situation.

Anytime there are highly charged circumstances placing the body in fear for its survival, the details are recorded into the DNA for future reference. If one's ancestor was stabbed in the back by a false friend in the middle of a fierce thunderstorm, today they may carry of Pattern that constantly warns them not to trust others or allow them to come physically close; they may prefer to always sit with their back against the wall and even become agitated whenever there is a powerful storm.

Most of us can learn to recognize when a Pattern is based on trauma; however, that is not always the case with those created by conditioning, which are more subtle. Conditioned Patterns are much like habits: so ingrained that we accept them as normal behavior without question. The servant who silently remains in the background, the retired fireman still on alert for the siren, the mother who always puts the needs of others before her own—these are all conditioned ways of behaving. Conditioning, like a computer program, can keep running long after its original purpose has ended.

Some of our conditioning is based on sociocultural customs and rules. For instance, a woman who wants to exercise by taking a walk around the block might experience a vague unease so disquieting that she is stopped from going out. Questioning herself, and knowing she lives in a safe area, she finds no fear of being attacked. In fact, she often sees others walking their dogs, or strolling with friends. Yet she cannot take a simple walk outside alone, and wonders why.

One possible explanation is that her body holds a conditioned Pattern set during the Victorian era, when it was considered socially unacceptable behavior for a single woman of a certain class to be seen walking alone—only servants and "streetwalkers" did that. In another example, the conditioning might have been set by certain cultural restrictions similar to ones that exist in Afghanistan, where even today it is forbidden for a female to be seen in public without a male escort.

If, in order to belong or feel accepted, a woman could not walk alone in public, her "survival" within her sociocultural community demanded she obey or suffer the consequences. Depending on the society, the punishment could range from mild ostracism to a public whipping. *This* is why her BodyMind stops her from taking a walk today.

Past conditioning in the body can also be purely physical, without necessarily being a Pattern. For example, if the body "remembers" having its feet bound in China, one may habitually stand with their toes curled under. A habit of waking up around 3:00 a.m. is common if one carries old memories of being required to attend sacred prayer rituals at that hour in the temple, convent, or monastery. This sleep disruption is especially common—more so for women than for men—in those who actively engage in spiritual practices.

Transmission: "The Renunciate"

This Transmission, taken for a fifteen-month-old boy diagnosed as autistic, offers the possibility that this affliction is connected to a series of lives involving severe lack of sensory stimulation.

This condition arises from a combination of factors: biological, sociological, and psychological. In its very essence it epitomizes that which Master Alignment is attempting to teach—that the body retains all past experiences of the entity and its ancestors in the DNA. If the information has a strong emotional component, it affects the body's biophysical composition. For example, fear releases certain chemicals that affect the body's endocrine system, triggering a "fight or flight" response. This reaction is based on the experiences of humanity's most primitive ancestors, and it still activates in the body today when a situation is perceived to be fearful.

We would examine the fear response of "flight," because that is what we find within this young boy's condition. There are three major ways one may "take flight": actually moving the body away from the cause of the fear; withdrawing or shattering one's awareness, as happens in dissociation; and running inward— retreating into a tight, high focus inside the self. The desired effect of all three is identical: the separation of self or consciousness from that which triggers survival fear. The form of flight one finds in autism is a "turning in," an extreme internal focusing, to the exclusion of most external stimuli.

Behavioral habit Patterns form in the DNA when there is a buildup of past-life or hereditary experiences, some of which may be connected to fear. In this child's case, Pattern responses have reached an extreme level, because they were set in several lifetimes in which he lived or worked in locations of great solitude, with little or no outside stimuli. These places included a dark cave, a prison cell, and an underground mining tunnel.

This child spent one entire lifetime as a Welsh coal miner whose working days began before sunrise and ended after sunset. He spent the intervening hours in the darkness of the tunnels. In another life, he was an extreme Renunciate, living as a religious hermit within a desolate cave, with no human or animal contact save small insects—upon which he obsessed, as they were his only companions.

Therefore, this child came into this life with heavy DNA imprinting around solitude, introspection, sensory deprivation, and survival fear. This combination almost requires him to respond to life by withdrawing from it. This is a flight into his darkened cave, cell, or tunnel, for therein can he find familiar surroundings and personal safety.

Because of the history imprinted in his DNA, his present body could not cope with the concentrated stimulation of sight, sound, color, texture, and smells of the modern world into which he was born. The sensory overload resulted in an immediate withdrawal of his consciousness. As a habit Pattern, it can be removed from the DNA and replaced with Light energy. This will then allow cellular memories from other nonreclusive lives to arise and replace those that now trigger his inward flight.

Spiritually, his parents agreed to take on this experience. It is only the more advanced Souls who are even allowed to volunteer for such a project. The rejoicing they felt at his birth was coupled with their Souls' ecstasy at being gifted with such a child. We remind them that there is no sin or failure on their part that caused this situation. Love and acceptance of the child will go a long way toward facilitating his clearing processes.

The Paternal Blessing

The most subtle form of conditioning occurs when something is missing from the life, and its absence is noted unconsciously. When we become so used to circumstances that they begin to take on a mantle of unquestioned "truth," it never even occurs to us to consider whether a problem exists not because something is in the way, but because something is lacking.

In a weekend Intensive, we worked with an entrepreneur who was dealing with issues hampering a business expansion. In the process, we uncovered an issue that affects many of us. His major problem did not involve the ability to create opportunities; it was difficulty in achieving financial success despite all his efforts. There was no question of his competence; however, he was deeply frustrated, because his hard work did not result in a commensurate abundance.

Intuitively the Guides reminded us that there is a direct connection between the ability to attract, keep, and expand one's financial resources and a feeling of acceptance by one's father. This information corresponds with other Transmissions stating that money is merely a symbol-of-a-symbol, the first layer of which is our feeling acceptable to others. (At the next highest level, money—along with sex and power—stands as a symbol for Love.)

Acceptance by the father is best expressed in the New Testament phrase, "This is my beloved son (child), in whom I am well pleased." This simple sentence has three very important aspects: the father's recognition/acknowledgment of the child as his own; an assertion that the child is loved; and an assurance that the father not only loves the child, he is also accepting of the child's behavior, personality, and achievements.

The Old Testament also gives a powerful example of the connection between wealth and paternal acceptance in Genesis

27 when Isaac bestows a blessing on his son Jacob: "God give thee of the dew of Heaven, and the fatness of the earth, and plenty of corn and wine..." And again in Genesis 28: "And God Almighty bless thee and make thee fruitful and multiply thee..." These Patriarchal Blessings are clearly blessings of abundance.

Unfortunately, the vast majority of humans—both male and female—have never received such a loving acknowledgment from their fathers, primarily because the Paternal Blessing has become a lost ritual. One's father could not pass it on because he never received it from his father, neither was his grandfather acknowledged and blessed by HIS father, and so on. Thus there is a great hunger within the human body and psyche for the Paternal Blessing's clear and unequivocal acceptance by one's father.

Because the information in the DNA can be traced back over thousands of years to our earliest ancestors, everyone's DNA contains a link to all the males in their paternal line. (This also includes the male side of the maternal line.) This means that we all still hold in our present body a DNA remnant of the last ancestor who possessed not only the knowledge of *how* to bestow the Paternal Blessing, he also had the *power* to do so. According to our teaching sources, we all have the ability to then "connect" with that ancestor and to invoke his activation of the Paternal Blessing for ourselves. By so doing we will also activate the blessing for everyone in our family line, beginning with that ancestor down to the present. Therefore, by invoking this Blessing, we can also heal our ancestral line at the same time.

To invoke the Paternal Blessing for yourself, sit quietly with your feet on the floor and pause for a moment to center your awareness in your body. State:

"I invoke the last ancestor in my ancestral line who had both the knowledge and the power to confer upon me the Paternal Blessing. I ask that the Paternal Blessing be bestowed upon me in this moment."

Next, visualize and/or sense a white, iridescent Light moving slowly from the top of your head down through your entire body until it is anchored into the earth. The Guides indicate that the Blessing is locked into the sacral area (this region of the body holds issues around feeling supported). As follow-up, they suggested receiving some type of body work—osteopathic, chiropractic, cranial sacral, even massage—to help the body fully "seed in" this energy, and to release any blocks that may hinder its full expression.

Do not entertain thoughts or beliefs of your unworthiness—remember that Jacob received a valid, binding Blessing although he gained it through trickery.

Oaths, Vows, and Promises

We are all familiar with vows in the context of the marriage ceremony and perhaps are less aware of the countless other vows we routinely make. Anytime we proclaim an oath or make an important promise—especially if an emotional charge is involved—these are recorded in our BodyMind. Although they may be long outdated, they still affect our lives. Simply saying, "I will always..." or "I will never..." is enough to create an on-going commitment that far outlives its purpose.

- A young man learns the reason he is having difficulty attracting a close relationship is because, as a Knight in the 14th century, he "pledged his troth" to a young woman. To his BodyMind, he is still engaged to her and, therefore, not presently available to be in a relationship.

- All warriors who made vows of revenge and retribution, may still be carrying repressed anger in their bodies. This rage is stored as "fuel" to keep their commitment alive until they fulfill their oath. Despite potential high blood pressure, they somehow know they cannot release the anger, because to do so would be to violate their internal code, which decrees "Death before dishonor."

- The grandmother who 60 years ago promised her young children she would "never leave them" now lies wasting away in a nursing home, while her body still holds her to her promise.

- At the end of the Civil War, many imitated Scarlett O'Hara by proclaiming, "As God is my witness, I will never be hungry again!" Does that contribute to their inability to eat moderately today? Kitchen cabinets filled to overflowing are one sign of past starvation, when we or our ancestors assuredly made a similar vow.

- The young Roman wife vows to wait for her beloved as he goes off to conquer the Gauls, suspecting she may never see him again. Today she has an inexplicable habit of gazing longingly out the window as if expecting someone to arrive. She also wonders why she is less than whole-hearted in her current relationship. There is a part of her still waiting for her centurian to return.

Spiritual Vows

In ancient times, temple initiates took vows similar to those of modern religious orders. These vows are still in the body and can affect us in unexpected ways, as these excerpts from two personal Transmissions illustrate:

Your fear of commitment also arises from the many lifetimes in which you sought to obtain knowledge within the temple. As one who loved learning, you were primarily motivated in those lives not by the desire to become more spiritual, but to be near the libraries which were housed in the temple. You were still required, however, to take the Priestess Vows of Poverty, Chastity, Obedience, and Silence.

As taught, Patterns become imprinted through trauma, conditioning, and vows. One who has taken the Vow of Chastity cannot give their heart to anyone but the God/Goddess. The term "virgin" means one who is "self-contained"; therefore, this vow required one to refrain from human intimacy, "saving oneself" for the goddess. Because your DNA still contains a record of these vows, today that imprinting will not allow you to attract a committed relationship—this is merely the body's way of helping you keep your ancient Vow of Chastity.

The Vow of Silence also relates to your Pattern: Under pain of death, this vow required one to withhold the sacred teachings from the uninitiated. If this vow were violated, both the teacher and uninitiated student were put to death. As someone who wants to be a teacher, do you not see how this would cause you to be afraid? What if you were not "sufficiently qualified" through Initiation? What if you inadvertently taught a doctrine that must remain secret? Your fear of death—while justified in those lifetimes, yet no longer valid today—prevents you from assimilating or sharing knowledge.

Another Transmission revealed information on additional fear-based beliefs engendered by the Vow of Silence:

This ancient Vow of Silence has created two blocks: one within your memory and the other in your psyche.

When one must not reveal "the secret" under pain of death, it generates an unconscious belief that one must withhold all-important information from others. Because you were afraid you might reveal the secrets inadvertently, as a prevention you developed a habit of being forgetful. If one forgets what they know, there is less danger of accidentally revealing what must remain hidden. Therefore, to your own consternation in the present, the more important a piece of information is, the more likely you will be to forget it.

In addition, one who has taken the Vow of Silence may experience psychological confusion: they start to believe the "secret" is about them—something that if known by others, would cause public humiliation or death. It is as if you yourself then become the secret. This makes you tend to avoid intimacy and reinforces your sense of isolation—a never-ending cycle of one Patterns feeding into another.

Know that the time for secrets has passed, and now is the time to reveal the Truth. We ask all those once trained and initiated into the Mysteries to come forward into the Light and to give of that Light into the world, so that through and in the Light all humanity may See, and truly Seeing, Know.

The effect of these vows can be ended by affirming:

> *"If, in any lifetime, I took Vows of Poverty, Chastity, Obedience, and Silence, I hereby rescind such vows for now and for all time."*

While not mentioned in these brief excerpts, the Vows of Poverty and Obedience can also create difficulties in the present. Today the Vow of Poverty translates as, "If I commit to my spiritual growth, then I cannot have wealth or possessions." Whether we have taken this vow, will become apparent when we start to show an interest in spiritual subjects—even simple meditation. That is when we might begin to see an inverse relationship develop between our spiritual growth and our ability to own property or have financial abundance.

The Vow of Obedience means that we cannot initiate actions or imbue our choices with personal power, because our BodyMind demands we wait for the High Priest/Priestess to tell us what we can or cannot do. This is why so many feel the constant need to appeal to their Guides for direction. We have learned that spiritual guidance is to be used in much the same way as we use road signs on the highway—as indications of what lies ahead if we take certain routes, not necessarily as a command to go in one direction or another.

The Healer's Oath

As the examples show, an untold number of vows, promises, and commitments are cluttering up our lives. Beyond those mentioned are hundreds more. Every time we emphatically swear an oath or make a promise, we are creating a potential Pattern that can unconsciously affect us or our descendants.

It may also be important for us to become aware of another vow—the Healer's Oath. This vow has far-reaching effects on anyone currently in the healing profession—*or who might ever have been.*

The Bible states: "Physician, heal thyself." While "The Wounded Healer" is a title given to the mythological Chiron, this can apply to many healers today. Some will see the truth in the assertion, "Healers make the worst patients." They might perform near miracles for others and yet are ineffective in healing themselves or those close to them. They may work long hours for minimal compensation and feel held down—"something" is hindering them, and they cannot see it, analyze it or affirm it away.

We first learned of the existence of the Healer's Oath while struggling to apply self-healing that was not working as well as it might. In frustration, we finally thought to ask and received the following inspired teaching, which revealed that our bodies were complying with an ancient oath.

During an unknown time in history, a group of powerful healers worked with spiritual healing energies. Because of their expertise and effectiveness, these healers were in great demand; however, they began to fear that sharing the energies with great numbers could deplete their personal resources. To preserve their own health and longevity, these healers decided to "save" some of the energy for themselves by limiting their practices.

Other healers, who disagreed with this decision, believed that withholding healing energies for personal enrichment was "unspiritual." They felt that anyone gifted with such abilities had a moral and ethical obligation to give away all the energies, keeping nothing for themselves. This second group of healers then created an oath, vowing never to benefit personally from spiritual healing energies. This oath later became part of many initiation ceremonies. Unfortunately, those who took this oath failed to realize its full and long-ranging effects.

Today, we can look at this issue with a greater under-standing regarding the nature of spiritual healing energies. Despite their apparent disagreement, these two positions were based on an identical misconception: that the energies could somehow be quantified and must, therefore, be limited in nature. This was not true then, neither is it true now. Spiritual healing energies are limitless; they can be shared and still be infinitely available for one's own use.

Even realizing this cognitively is not enough however. Because this oath is imprinted in the DNA, our bodies still honor it. Therefore, to be able to move away from its limiting effects, we must also rescind this oath in the same way we rescind the spiritual vows:

"If, in any lifetime, I, or anyone on my behalf, took oaths preventing the personal use and benefit of spiritual healing energies, I hereby rescind such oaths for now and for all time."

The Causal Moment

Although new Patterns may appear in our lives at any time, we are most often challenged by those imprinted hundreds if not thousands of years ago, at a point called the "Causal Moment." Generally defined, this is an emotionally charged event so powerful that its elements were seared into the body consciousness for all time. The body will have such a strong need to retain the "lesson" of the experience that it is impossible to dislodge the memory now in the DNA using normal means such as positive thinking, or cognitive/behavioral therapy.

In addition, the body may encode a particularly important lesson in such a way that it now has an overly broad application. In one Intensive, a woman wanted to address her addiction to smoking. Her judgments, guilt, and even shame over having this "nasty habit" were probably harder on her body than her actual cigarette use, which was minimal. Her emotions were far beyond what one might expect, and we wondered why. It became clear when we asked for the underlying Causal Moment.

We were shown a brief scene of a sailor on watch aboard an ancient warship. It was the dead of night, and as he stood at the railing in the pitch darkness, he lit his pipe. In that moment, the enemy was able to see, target, and subsequently destroy the ship. Thus, a mere flicker of light in an otherwise dark seascape resulted in the destruction of the ship and all aboard her. The immense guilt this woman felt for smoking was really connected to the guilt from that experience combined with the fear that she could still cause the death of hundreds.

In attempting to glean the greatest amount of Wisdom from this experience, however, the BodyMind had expanded lesson learned in the original incident. Today, as it is encoded into her BodyMind, the expanded message of her Pattern is, "If I show my Light, many others will be killed." She is a powerful spiritual teacher, yet as a result of her Pattern, she somehow feels she must hide her Light (through the use of "impure" substances and the "sin" of being addicted to nicotine) so that she does not inadvertently cause the death of others. By understanding and releasing the fear and guilt established in the Causal Moment aboard the warship, she will then be able to allow her Light to reach and heal untold numbers of people.

We do not want to remove all encoding from our DNA. Many times the information imprinted there can prevent us from harm. In order to survive, all humans need a healthy respect for the elements, for fire, water, wind, as well as for heights, vicious animals, and even traffic. We consider a fear to be a Pattern when it operates in a manner that is more than merely protective of life and limb— it is hindering our ability to live and express to our highest capabilities.

Transmission: "Survivor's Guilt"

More complex Patterns may involve several layers of loss or pain. As a rule the Causal Moment in which this type of Pattern was set up will be very intense, as the following Transmission, done for a nine-year-old girl with leukemia illustrates.

Certain health conditions are manifestations of guilt generated in the past by great traumas that held dire consequences for themselves or their loved ones. The critical event—or Causal Moment—most often associated with the disease of leukemia usually involves a vast amount of bloodshed as well.

The Causal Moment for this child happened in a prior lifetime, when her entire village-clan was massacred by the neighboring tribe, and she—a female in her early teens at the time—was the sole survivor. She was not in any way responsible for this devastation, yet she internalized an immense amount of guilt as a way of coping with her loss. Later, she began to confuse this guilt with "fault" as in, "If I feel so guilty, what must I have done (or not done) to cause the loss of all those whom I loved?" Today this is called "survivor's guilt."

In the present life she was also been born into a large extended family—a village-sized clan. Her illness was partially triggered by this fact alone, because it serves as both a metaphor for the trauma and as a reminder never again to bring harm to her family. Therefore, today she harbors strong self-doubts and continually questions the "rightness" of her actions. She fears forgetting something important, and she worries that her loved ones will suffer because of something she may do inadvertently.

While neither her acts nor her omissions were the cause of the original trauma, the event still has repercussions in her BodyMind.

This Causal Moment marked the beginning of her journey to learn the meaning of true responsibility, which we do not define as blame. Along her journey she has earned and integrated certain positive characteristics: attentiveness to details, precision in her perceptions, valuing family relationships, and thoroughness. The Causal Moment created certain "needs" as well, especially the need to avoid making any mistakes harmful to herself or her family. She has little tolerance for those who are careless or inattentive. In truth these are judgments against traits that belong to her unconscious or "shadow" side and are also a result of her survivor's guilt.

There are several other reasons she has chosen to manifest this health condition in this life. The first relates to her immediate reactions at the time of the Causal Moment. Because she was horrified by the sight of the blood and mutilation, her body imprinted this memory as an automatic repulsion response—so much so that she even rejected her own blood. This rejection response is her body's attempt to shield itself from bringing the original horror to full consciousness.

This disease also acts as a powerful reminder of her need to prevent such a trauma this lifetime. To avoid repeating an intensely painful event, one will make vows and promises such as "I will never again..." or "I will always..." while willingly accepting any sacrifices required to keep these. Although made sometime around the Causal Moment, these vows and promises are still operating in the life through the body consciousness. To ensure she will remember never to cause harm to others, she offers her own blood as a "sacrifice." She had vowed, "I will never (*again*) be the cause of any bloodshed. I fear being responsible (*again*) for the loss of those I love. Therefore, I reject all forms of blood (the vow) even if this calls for me to suffer the loss of my own blood" (the sacrifice).

In addition, she has a driving need to compensate for her

perceived "sin" in the Causal Moment. This is compounded by her confusion what she did or did not do that was sinful; hence, she does not know how to atone for it. If she had stolen a sum of money, she could give a similar sum to charity as a way to achieve balance. How can she atone for an unknown act or omission which resulted in the bloody massacre of so many she loved except by "dying a thousand times"?

Many members of her current family also carry a DNA imprinted predisposition for self-blame and guilt; thus, this is partially a hereditary Pattern as well as a personal one. Part of her Soul's mission for this life is to be an instrument to help her family heal this Pattern. She made a commitment to manifest the hereditary self-blame and guilt in her own body through this disease. As she learns to understand all the purposes behind her disease, she will begin to realize she is capable of fulfilling her personal goal of "saving her village-clan" (this is a survivor's deep desire to restore them back to life) by allowing the outdated guilt to be removed from her own body.

To process all of this information with a goal toward healing, we recommend she be assisted to understand and accept that:

- This event, or one like it, actually happened in a distant time in history, whether to her or to one of her ancestors.
- It was indeed horrifying and traumatic—to state otherwise would not be the truth.
- It was natural for her to experience survivor's guilt, grief, anger, pain, and an enormous sense of helplessness afterward.
- Therefore, she internalized all these emotions; for lifetimes she believed herself to be at fault for this event.
- She was in no way responsible for the disaster through any word, deed, or omission. *This is critical for her to accept.*

- The Causal Moment triggered her to embark on a journey through many lifetimes to atone for her perceived wrongs. It also created an intense need to bring healing to her family.
- Throughout this journey she has acquired gifts, talents, knowledge, and abilities she might not otherwise have had.
- Despite any fear to the contrary, she is incapable of causing severe harm to her current "village-clan" through any careless thought, word, deed, or omission, because of all the wisdom she has acquired since the time of the Causal Moment.
- She can heal her family of its tendency to hold unspecified guilt by being willing to release her own—thus fulfilling, ironically, both her desire to atone and her Soul's Purpose.

If she can gently progress through these understandings to the final realization that she carries no blame for the events in the Causal Moment, she will be able to heal many others throughout her life, through either traditional medicine or alternative means. What truly matters is not the method she uses; it is the understanding that *accepting ownership of her own innocence is her greatest healing tool.*

Recognizing Patterns

To be able to clear our Patterns, we must learn to recognize when they are operating. Generally, a Pattern can be described as a "fear of..." or a "need to..." It is important to remember, however, fear often masks itself in many different disguises—as worry, anxiety, grief, and guilt.

All "need tos" are directly fear-based. We "need to" breathe because we know an inability to do so will lead to death; in the same way our need to have food, clothing, and shelter are based on survival. This is merely basic self-preservation, and we do not want to eliminate this level of information from the body. However, a "need to be right" might be based on a long outdated fear of losing our lives if we are found to be wrong. It is fine to *want* to be right, especially if we have a job that requires us to be as accurate as possible. When we use the phrase "need to," we mean that it has become an obsession beyond the normal requirements of the situation. A "need to" might be felt as an inner urgency that creates stress in the body. Generally, emotional stress is likely to relate to fear Patterns.

A Pattern is definitely operating when we experience a series of similar incidents causing the same pain or blockage. If one fears being abandoned in relationships, for example, and has felt "abandoned" by a parent, friend, or lover, a Pattern exists. The same applies to repetitious behavior that makes us act in self-defeating ways or causes problems in our work, self-expression, or relationships, to name a few.

Article: "The Step of Awareness"

The following is from a newsletter article written by Richard Rylander describing various physical and emotional reactions signaling when we might be in a Pattern.

For many, the most difficult step in clearing Patterns has been the step of recognizing them. Perhaps this is because it often requires developing new consciousness about ourselves and seeing where we have constructed fear-based limits.

If we allow ourselves to pay attention to what is happening in our bodies, the rage or fear that often indicates we are in a Pattern can be recognized by its ferocity. There will be emotional upset far beyond what the present moment calls for. There can be three types: angry rage—the "I could just kill them" feelings; suppressed rage in the form of depression, sadness, bitterness, denial, and withdrawal; or the passive expression of resentment, which wants others to feel guilt or regret. These reactions are red flags that we are dealing with a Pattern.

Look also for the urgency, for the need to escape or the need to prevail and be right. The need to escape a situation as soon as possible is the helpless "Victim" side of a Pattern. The intransigent, self-righteous, defensive attitude— "I am not open to new information or negotiation here. I'm right and that's the end if it!"—is the opposite, or "Hero" side. This part of us has made its sacrifices, and vows to keep from ever again being victimized.

Paying attention to the body in such moments, one will notice a rising up of adrenaline, bringing with it an increased heart rate and either more rapid breath or holding of the breath—even though the triggering event might be a simple criticism from our boss. Fear reactions such as these are a signal that our body has brought up the holographic history of a Pattern—including the original trauma of the Causal Moment. These reactions are invariably based on the ego/body's outdated belief that the present situation is a threat to its survival. This is the time we can most easily spot a Pattern, because, our body's physical and emotional reaction is far beyond what the present situation merits.

Those of us who have a tendency to "go out of our bodies" as a defense may suspect that we have triggered a Pattern when any or all of the following happen: We cannot feel our feet or legs, we become easily confused, or our sight or hearing is less acute. Feeling anxious, irritable and/or depressed for an hour or more when circumstances do not warrant it can be another clue we have triggered a Pattern. Ongoing emotional crises in any intimate relationship are sure signs we're in Pattern City.

Patterns are characterized by unavoidable either/or choices—win or lose, fight or flight, ideal perfection or shameful failure. Thus feeling "shameful failure" would be the Victim position and "ideal perfection" the Hero, who has worked to be as far removed as possible from that shameful failure. This is an example of the phrase, "the impact of opposites is the same." Both sides of the either/or choice mean living in reaction to the Pattern. The Victim is the "fear of" side of the issue, and the Hero is the "need to" side.

When we can name the Pattern as "a fear of..." or "the need to...," we have recognized it. As we name the Pattern, we can then choose to clear it, which allows us to abandon blame and take responsibility; giving us the power to make changes, to collapse the either/or polarity, to release the beliefs and fear from our body, and, finally, to stop repeating its old habits.

Transmission
"All in the Family: Shared Patterns"

This Transmission shows that while the same fear may be common to several family members, it can express itself as a variety of "need tos," thus creating conflict.

Fear Patterns generally will be at the root of most relationship disharmonies. Within close families especially, there will be a web of interrelated Patterns tying one person to another. In this family, for instance, one family member needs constant outside reassurance, based on an underlying fear that they are not "good enough," while another has a need to find fault in others, because they can only feel good enough if everyone else is worse than they are. The irony is that each person has an identical fear-based Pattern: that they will never be good enough. Clearly, there is a crisis in the making!

In this particular family, most of its members were attracted to the genetic inheritance of the biological line because each individually had a similar, well-developed belief in personal unworthiness. What differs from person to person within the family is the manner of expressing the "need to" that arises from the shared fear. It is the dynamic of how the individual egos have chosen to express the Pattern—their "need tos"—that creates conflict among the various family members.

The first person needs to receive constant praise, recognition, and assurances from those around them. Because this need is based on a fear Pattern, it will be insatiable; that is, it can never reach a level where the person will believe they are truly good enough. In their case, this Pattern—as all fear-based needs—will call for constant affirmation, accolades, and recognition from others. It may also manifest as self-aggrandizement or bragging.

The greatest difficulty with this type of fear Pattern is that there is no qualitative or quantitative measure by which one can ever be certain they have fulfilled their goal. "Good enough," as this might be defined for the Priestess in the temple, often meant a life of "perfection," disallowing for any sin, or even simple mistakes. One was expected to spend every minute in a state of absolute purity of mind, body, and spirit. Such a standard of perfection is an impossibility; however, this Pattern will still prod one to live by it. Therefore, the only result is "failure." The personal sense of guilt or impurity that flows from not having achieved the state of perfection then requires one to compensate by finding a means to feel good about oneself. One major way is to convince oneself they are "better than" others; hence, one will need effusive compliments to get the feeling one is "special" and, for a moment, assuage the negative feelings generated by the Pattern.

Another way to fulfill this same goal is to find fault with everyone else, demeaning others in order to elevate oneself to a position of "specialness." One who cannot use honey to sweeten their sense of self may choose vinegar to sour the sense of self in others, and by comparison feel sweeter. This method of making oneself feel good enough is also insatiable. In actuality, they do not realize that, in criticizing others, they are projecting all their "sins" and failures onto those around them. The need to find fault with others will grow until no one can ever satisfy the standard of perfection needed to stop the criticism by the one holding the Pattern. There is an ever greater need to throw off onto others what one cannot own about oneself. In addition, the length of time one can feel better about themselves—because they have found others "less than" themselves—also becomes shorter, as the need to criticize grows ever stronger. Thus, they fall into a habit of criticizing those around them.

There is a third variation of this same fear Pattern. This is the need to overachieve. Here, one turns all the criticism onto oneself and then attempts to assuage the resulting negative feelings by seeking a level of "perfection" through accomplishing more. This need is also insatiable; because today's successes will be discounted tomorrow, one must constantly struggle to overachieve to prove one is good enough. There is still the same problem: no standards or guidelines to assist one in knowing when they have finally fulfilled their goal, except the overbroad, vague, and illusory concept of "perfection."

Other family members may then perceive this success as a challenge to them; because this variation of the Pattern requires comparison. The "successful one" may not need to receive praise or criticize others without cause; yet, because of their achievements, they may seem more elevated than the others—who must now struggle even harder using their "need for praise," or "need to find fault." It is a never-ending cycle creating interfamily "dis-ease."

To become free of an insatiable need or unachievable goal (with this Pattern, even "successes" add up to failure in the end), one must be willing to release the fear Pattern. Then and only then can one find true fulfillment and self-worth. Releasing the Pattern collapses the sense of hierarchy, allowing each family member to feel good enough in themselves without comparison to anyone else.

For those who are willing, we suggest they work to recognize and stop this Pattern within themselves; this will also benefit everyone in the family who carries the same fear.

A practical way to facilitate clearing is to use the Self-Forgiveness exercise. This process asks one to first become aware when a Pattern appears—in this case, when any form of internal self-criticism arises. Realize one's ego/body is unnecessarily feeling bad about what one is currently doing or thinking (or has mistakenly done or failed to do in the past). At first, it may be difficult to become aware of the self-judgment; this realization may occur minutes or hours later. That is unimportant; the process still works if one undertakes the remaining steps once they do become aware. Next, say, "I do not need to feel bad about this mistake, omission, or 'wrong.' Instead I choose to keep the wisdom it offers me, and I release ALL the pain, guilt, and fear attached to this memory." Last, see a bubble bursting—this bubble represents the illusions created by the painful emotions. What remains is Love and wisdom.

When the psyche and the Soul see one is willing to release guilt for being less than perfect, it will offer other long-held memories for added clearing. One must do the release with each memory until they can actually sense there is nothing in their life for which they feel shame or regret.

After this release, one will be able to recognize the wisdom contained within each formerly "painful" moment and even find that "mistakes or errors" can be welcomed for their educational value. What also drops automatically from the life is the insatiable "need to": the need for constant praise or recognition, the need to criticize others to feel better about oneself, or the need to drive oneself to overachieve.

Then a miracle occurs: one receives compliments and praise, another feels joy in finding "rightness" in others, and the third accomplishes more with less effort. The outcome is guaranteed if one is willing to clear this Pattern.

Effects of Patterns

Every story in this book illustrates the many effects of Patterns. Even the brief examples offered up to this point illustrate how they affect us on the physical, emotional, mental, and spiritual levels. We frequently point out that the information imprinted as "truth" within the BodyMind may be out of alignment with our rational mind, our heart's desires, or our spiritual ideals, thus blocking our present ability to achieve our goals.

The information in the DNA can and will overrule all other efforts if the BodyMind determines *for any reason* that its physical survival is at stake.

Applying its memory of past emotional/physical experiences, our BodyMind can actually stop us from being who we truly are— even when our desires are strong. The Teacher who cannot teach, the Actor who cannot get a role, the promising Athlete who cannot get out of his slump—all of these may be the effects of hidden Patterns impervious to mind-altering techniques.

We have seen hundreds of cases where one's fear Patterns are the last remaining obstacle to living one's full potential or achieving one's Soul Purpose in this life.

Whenever the BodyMind perceives a threat—valid or not—it will set off an "alarm" by triggering fear-based emotions ranging from worry to outright terror, as discussed in prior chapters. Unfortunately, if the threat is not real, we are stopped from going forward even when there is no actual danger, and we do not understand why this has happened.

Letter: "The Prisoner"

What follows is a written response to a prison inmate who was less than a year from being paroled. He had mentioned certain fears that worried him: that he would die in prison before he was released, and that his imprisonment was part of an unknown karmic debt. Lastly, he questioned why he so often felt deceived by others.

All three of these concerns—your fear of dying, your "karmic debt," and being deceived by others—are connected. They arise from a single traumatic past-life event, which occurred sometime in the Middle Ages when, as the trusted teacher of the royal children at court, you suffered because of others' envy.

While this experience is part of your present DNA, it will be easier to refer to "him" in the third person to differentiate between the present and the past.

This teaching position in the court afforded him close access to members of the royal family. However, others resented his position and set out to discredit him in the eyes of the monarch. They were able to accomplish this through treachery and lies, such as repeating his words out of context. They convinced the king that the teacher was fomenting treason by subverting the royal children. Believing the envious, the king immediately had the teacher banished from the court and the castle grounds.

His sudden reversal of fortune came as an immense shock; he was not even given an explanation for his banishment. Because he had always lived within the castle walls and was unskilled in any other trade or craft, the teacher was incapable of surviving in the outside world. He soon perished, never understanding why he had been so abruptly expelled. Therefore, in this life you have a belief imprinted in your DNA: that you are incapable of supporting yourself in the world.

As a teacher in the royal court, he lived in a self-contained environment, and this was the only home he knew. The massive stone walls surrounding the heavily defended castle made him feel safe and secure. Everyone seemed to be part of an extended family, all their physical needs were provided for, and there was a strong hierarchical system in which he had a fixed position.

Today you are in prison, where all your basic needs are provided by the state. Ironically, you were placed in this impenetrable, highly defended institution by "the Court." This is not a coincidence; it was as close as you could get to living in a castle. Secure, defended stone walls equal "home" to you.

Your present fear is not that you will die in prison before you are paroled, the real fear is that you will die *if you leave it*. Historically, because the castle was a self-contained city, most never left it, neither did they feel the need to do so. Their safety and very survival depended on staying within the castle walls. To be suddenly be cast out of this environment was a virtual death sentence.

Notice how your fears around "dying" have been growing in intensity the closer your parole becomes a reality. Your BodyMind is trying to sound the alarm that you will die if you are released into the outside world. The body does not live in time—it honestly believes that the trauma you experienced in the Middle Ages will happen again if you find yourself outside the "castle" walls. Your mind and heart desire freedom, yet the BodyMind, "remembering" what happened centuries ago, still responds in fear. You have decided this fear is a warning that you will die in prison—your Pattern says the opposite.

While it is true that we all have karmic debts, your need to uncover your "great and horrible crime" is a lingering remnant of the teacher's not understanding why he was cast out to die. His "crime" was that of being envied by others. Envy is classified as a major sin because it "kills." Jealousy is wanting what another has, while envy seeks to destroy them for having it. Those who find themselves to be the object of others' envy only rarely perceive the resentment directed toward them until it is too late—they are blindsided.

Family members or others in close proximity, such as co-workers, are those who most commonly envy another's success. They hide their resentment, sometimes even from themselves, until it unexpectedly explodes into overt action. The one who is envied then laments, "Why me? What did I do to deserve this?" They lie in the dust, everything they own—their home, reputation, livelihood, and close relationships—destroyed or taken from them, while they try vainly to figure out their "crime."

The teacher's expulsion was so sudden he had no opportunity to defend himself. Remember, his detractors used deception to turn the royal family against him. All our fears are based on real events that happened in the past; therefore, we only fear what we have already experienced. The fear of "being deceived" clearly arises from prior experiences in which one experienced deception by others. You are overly vigilant today because *he* was naive and unsuspecting. His enemies' resentment caught the teacher unawares, which only added to his shock and pain. He/you vowed never to allow this to happen again, and you support this vow in the present by being suspicious of others' motivations.

Along with the fear, shock, and vows encoded in the DNA, other issues keep these Patterns locked in the body: the ego's *identification* with the trauma, as well as feelings of resentment against those who were envious or deceptive. The egoic identification with resentment provides the "glue" that holds fear Patterns in the DNA. If, as in this situation, the BodyMind constantly broadcasts the message, "Look what they did to me: they deceived me. I am

Deceived," the world replies, "Message received: *Who you are* is 'one-who-is-deceived.' Therefore, others must deceive you to support this identity." Today you will tend to attract those who will deceive you.

We teach that those who love us must and will bring us our Patterns; this is their answer to the BodyMind's "request." In Love, they grant what we have unconsciously asked. For example, anyone with this particular Pattern could have a relationship with an otherwise loyal, honorable person, who will *have to deceive them*. This is how powerful our Patterns are in affecting the behavior of those around us. By eliminating the Pattern, we also change the way others act toward us. When we willingly release the Pattern's victim identity, miracles begin to occur in all our relationships. This happens because our BodyMind no longer broadcasts messages attracting those who must bring us our Patterns.

Please contemplate the possibility that this past-life trauma is behind your fears and concerns. A willingness to integrate this information will make a huge difference in your success as a future parolee.

Transmission: "Avoiding the Barbarian Within"

This Transmission, received on behalf of a therapist who also presents workshops on aging, demonstrates how outdated fear Patterns can prevent us from recognizing and fulfilling our true Soul Purpose work.

We start with an image of a small, rustic village, and of a young girl-child. She has not yet reached puberty and is the delight of her rather elderly parents. She is an only child, and knows that she is cherished and loved; this makes her feel open, accepted, and loving of others around her, for Love always begets Love.

Her family's life is simple, as are their wants and needs. There is a time, however, when this life comes to a crushing halt: an invasion from the north in which their village is overrun by barbarians. Her parents and many others are killed right before her eyes, while she stands there in fear, grief, and horror. Given the opportunity she might then have tried to cause her own death—such were her terror and revulsion. She is spared because the invaders see her as a "valuable asset"—one that can bear children to expand the invaders' numbers.

As the band departs the village, she leaves behind the only life she has ever known and all who love and cherish her. Village after village, she is also forced to witness the same destruction and death. The deaths of the elderly especially bother her, for they continually replay in her mind the senseless and violent deaths of her parents.

She is no more than a slave, and one roughly treated at that, yet this actually has the effect of strengthening her character instead of weakening her. While she longs to flee her captors, she has no illusions of being rescued or escaping, and she decides to do whatever she can to make her life and those of the other prisoners more endurable.

The life is extremely difficult, and their treatment of her is deplorable. Although she is never perceived as "human" by her captors, her parents' early love has given her a firm sense of her own value and identity. This certainty buoys her spirit and helps her to survive. Yet, because of lack of sufficient food and shelter, her body if not her spirit is weak; and she dies when they are snowed in as the band attempts a mountain crossing. She is not afraid of death—in truth she sees it as the escape she so longs for; all the killings she has witnessed also inured her to it. She has nothing to live for, and welcomes death when it comes. She even sees her death as a way to retaliate against her captors—she realizes it is depriving them of something they want.

From this one short life, many gifts and abilities serve her well today, including the ability to make difficult situations easier for others. There are also Patterns that must be addressed if she is to be fully successful in using these gifts to their highest advantage. Because the Causal Moment was so traumatic and occurred so suddenly, disrupting every aspect of her life, today she carries a fear of the "unexpected" in her body. She also has a need to anticipate the outcome of events, to project herself into all possible "alleyways of dark probabilities." She never again wants to be caught in a situation where "invading hordes" can swoop down and destroy everything she loves.

This Pattern is similar to the Warrior's need to be vigilant; however, it is locked in her body as a memory belonging to a small, helpless child. This difference is critical, because the girl-child's fear is often still running her life today. She constantly feels a need to prevent the "darkness" or the "unknown" from taking everything away. This compels her to always over-prepare and to have contingency plans for all negative possibilities. However, because it is part of a fear Pattern, this "need to" is obsessive; no amount of planning, preparation, or "shoring up the defenses" will ever be enough to satisfy it. There is wisdom hidden by this fear: a highly developed ability to be aware of aspects within a complex situation others might miss.

The Pattern also shows itself in her belief that "loss" will follow every "good"; hence, she is careful not to let herself experience unbridled joy, believing deep sorrow and grief will automatically follow. In that lifetime she had no time or opportunity to grieve the loss of her beloved parents or the life she had known, and that child's grief still sits unresolved within her.

A part of her clearly recognizes these feelings and does not know how to release them. The small girl-child "knows" that if she allows the grief to come forward, it will overwhelm and consume her in its full intensity—she is as certain of this as she is that the sun rises in the morning. To protect herself and those she loves from this emotional torrent, she feels that it is better to restrain and control all intense emotions within her body. She does all this out of Love, for she also greatly fears that her emotions— due to their primal nature—are capable of turning her into a "barbarian" should she release them. Remember, this Pattern was set by a very young child who experienced destruction and horror. She does not fear the emotions themselves, rather she fears their depth, because she recognizes and believes in their ability to destroy.

Having vowed never to become like the barbarians, she represses her emotional expression, and thereby sacrifices a very powerful and effective part of herself. At a simple, innocent place within herself, she truly believes that her emotions could sweep her uncontrollably along to a point where she would harm others— just as the barbarians swept in and destroyed all she loved. She prides herself on her ability to "know and control"; however, she does not fully realize how difficult this is on her body.

She has mentioned issues with her blood pressure; this also relates to her fear of expressing the depth of her emotions. She has held these intense emotions in so well that they threaten to become the very thing she fears: a "barbaric explosion." Emotional repression has a direct effect on the body's nervous system, and nerve impulse messages are part of the system that regulates blood pressure.*

Today, in her work with the elderly, she still seeks to heal the loss of her beloved parents from that lifetime. She has always loved and honored those in their senior years. This is another healthy attribute from that past life, yet her unexpressed grief and guilt over the loss of her parents overshadow this gift. The child in her believes that she should have prevented their deaths. While this would have been unreasonable under those circumstances, it is wholly reasonable to the mind of the child. Guilt over not having saved her parents has stayed with her, along with a need to atone for having failed.

This trauma was the beginning of a Soul journey that has led to her present role in the world. It is from this seminal lifetime that she set out to "rescue" her loved ones and to make reparations for her failures. This was an honorable goal, one that has motivated her for many subsequent lifetimes. What hampers its fulfillment is the fact her inner child feels neither healed nor forgiven for her perceived "failures." When she has cleared these beliefs, her love and all her hidden gifts will bloom, for they will no longer be fettered by unnecessary guilt.

In addition, her Soul is preparing her to take on another role, one in which she will be more actively involved in protecting and securing certain rights for the elderly. This role needs her full "arsenal" of power, which is blocked by two fears: that she must use all her present skills to protect herself and her loved ones from potential unknown invaders, and that she must never allow her emotions to be fully unleashed.

Left uncleared, these beliefs will effectively prevent her from using the full scope of her abilities in such a role. In addition, her Pattern would immediately attract an overpowering "barbaric horde" in the form of governmental and medical bureaucracies over which she would feel powerless. Her outdated beliefs would invite power struggles she would be incapable of handling as long as her Patterns were present. Who she is in truth is more than capable of advocating for the elderly; it is the young girl-child who would feel overwhelmed and fearful. Hence, she must consciously integrate the child's outdated fears and release her old vows.

Ironically, she knows herself to be powerful and this, too, is a gift that evolved beginning in that lifetime; however, she diverts too much of her power into repression. This does not mean she is to explode at every small thing—far from it. The point we keep emphasizing is her inner girl-child is still holding control over her emotions. Today her head and heart know that she will not destroy those she loves; thus, the Patterns in her DNA no longer align with her present awareness. This misalignment must be addressed. She must put aside the child's fear and replace it with the adult's ability to express in suitable ways and at appropriate times. If it means she displays justifiable anger, it cannot harm anyone or anything—except the lie.

In her Soul Identity, she is a Warrior. Because she fears that she will become like the barbarians, out of Love and a need to protect others she hides this identity from herself. She would rather "deny herself" than cause devastation to those she loves. For this reason it is critical she understands that the role of the modern Warrior is to challenge the lie—it is not to harm others. In this she can be very effective. She has powerful qualities in her "arsenal": her emotions, her depth of caring and love, the intensity of her determination, and the passion of her convictions. These are her weapons against the darkness, and only her Patterns prevent her from skillfully applying them.

Author's Note: in 1992, I was told intuitively, "Cholesterol is not a function of diet or lack of exercise. Cholesterol is the result of an inability to feel and express the emotions." It was further explained that, while the heart is the center of the emotional body, the veins are the "highways and byways," symbolizing the channels by which one communicates feelings. If one cannot express emotions—positive or negative—the veins will exhibit this through "gridlock" or clogging.

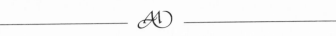

Part Two:
Matrices and Archetypes

Introduction

As a species, human beings hold an incredible number of fear Patterns in their BodyMinds. For teaching purposes, we have organized all Patterns into seven major divisions, or **Matrices**, representing our basic human needs and goals: Survival, Power, Nurturing, Knowledge, Creativity, Spirituality, and Mastery.

Each Matrix contains several **Archetypes,** which represent the *major experiences* all humans share. In actuality, every Pattern is part of the human condition, therefore it can be under any of the Matrices. We place the Grief Pattern in the Nurturing Matrix; however, all who lose a loved one are vulnerable to this Pattern.

Archetypes are not Patterns. If one says, "I have a Teacher Pattern," they really mean they have fears arising from their teaching experiences. When we eliminate the Pattern, we do not also reject its inner wisdom—the ability to be a teacher, in this instance. Our goal is to use the knowledge, gifts, and talents harvested from our experience while removing any blocks.

The older the Soul, the more likely one is to have had experiences in most of the major Archetypes—as Refugee, Warrior, King/Queen, Caretaker, Teacher, Artist and Priest/Priestess. This means they will also carry a wide range of Patterns in their DNA. The last Matrix represents Mastery on the Earth plane, thus fewer people have touched into its issues.

Archetypes differ from **Soul Identities,** which remain constant throughout many lifetimes, despite the nature of one's experiences. A Warrior Soul Identity may also have experience as a Refugee or Priest, besides having fought on the battlefield.

First Matrix: Survival —"The Pioneer"

Second Matrix: Power —"The King/Warrior"

Third Matrix: Nurturing — "The Caretaker"

Fourth Matrix: Knowledge —
"The Scholar/Teacher"

Fifth Matrix: Creativity —"The Artist"

Sixth Matrix: Spirituality —"The Priest/Priestess"

Seventh Matrix: Mastery — "The Merlin"

The Survival Matrix

The first Matrix deals with all basic life-and-death issues—anything that affected our ability to survive in a particular time and place. In actuality, all fears eventually can be traced back to our fear of dying; therefore, all Patterns are ultimately rooted in this Matrix.

There are several Archetypes included in the Survival Matrix: the Immigrant/Pioneer, the Refugee, and even the Bastard. All have several factors in common: loss of an identity, feelings of not belonging, material loss or deprivation, and great hardship. These are only some of the examples we might place under this Matrix.

The Immigrant/Pioneer gave up their known world to settle a new one, leaving behind old identities, security, and often loved ones in the process. Because the majority of our ancestors settled here from other countries, most of us carry a vestige of this Archetype and, to a greater or lesser degree, issues associated with fears that equate "leaving home" with loss or grief.

The situation is even more difficult for Refugees, who are forced by calamity, war, or natural disaster to flee for their very lives, often with only the clothes on their backs. Usually they are relocated to an area where they are not wanted and are looked down upon. It does not matter that they may have been a prosperous business owner in their own land; as refugees they have nothing to show for it—no home, no money, no title. All this is combined with knowing they do not belong and that their very presence is resented; neither does their name or reputation mean anything. Thus, there is a loss of personal identity. We see the Refugee Archetype almost daily on the evening news—in Africa, the Balkans, and wherever there has been a major disaster.

It is safe to say this is the most universal of all Archetypes. Hidden somewhere within everyone's DNA are personal or ancestral memories of having lived—even for a short time—as a Refugee. This is important to remember, because the fears associated with Refugee experiences trigger profound survival terror.

We also include in this Archetype those who were born out of wedlock and labeled "Bastard." In many countries, to be called a bastard meant that one had no right to a name, no right to wealth, and therefore, no right to marry in some instances. They may feel as if they even have no right to belong. It is interesting to speculate whether those who strive so hard to "make a name for themselves"—and when they do succeed, name everything after themselves—might carry a certain amount of this Pattern in their DNA.

If our Soul asks us to address fear Patterns in order to prepare for the next level of spiritual advancement, our body will begin to bring forward any past remembrances around survival struggles and any fears around material deprivation. The objective is to extract and integrate the wisdom earned and learned from these fear-based experiences so that they need not recur in the present life.

Those who went through the loss of all they owned because of disaster or having started over in a new land possess an incredible ability to survive under any and all circumstances. From their past hardships they have all the hard-earned wisdom, information, and character traits needed; these strengths are simply hidden beneath their outdated fear reactions.

Transmission: "The Tribal Outcast"

This Transmission was received for a West Coast businesswoman. It tells a powerful story—one that may resonate at a deep level with many who are also succeeding in the world, and wondering why, beneath it all, they are still so afraid.

This is a story of one who, although the daughter of an important tribal leader, was made an outcast because she was stricken with leprosy. While there was no name for this disease in that distant time, the tribe's people recognized her condition as highly contagious, physically disfiguring, and fatal.

When the signs of the disease became clear in her body, she was driven from her village, and all that she owned was destroyed. As was also the custom, her name and identity were obliterated from the tribe's oral history. The people did all this out of the belief that the "gods" themselves had branded her as "unwanted." The tribe banished her because they neither wanted to be infected with this dreadful disease nor could they risk incurring Divine wrath for associating with one whom the gods themselves had rejected.

This young woman had seen another who was marked by the disease and then banished from the tribe several months before; therefore, she immediately felt deep fear and despair over her plight. She knew there would be no one to comfort her in her suffering, or to nurse her in her dying days. She felt profound abandonment, and this rejection has severely affected her for many lifetimes. Similar experiences in later lifetimes only added to the pain from her experience as an outcast. All these are seared into her body's DNA and contribute to her overwhelming feelings of rejection.

Her body contains many intense issues around not belonging,

being punished for circumstances beyond her control, and feeling unsupported and alone if she is in a crisis. She tends to hide her problems from others, believing that they might then judge her to be "marked" by the gods. Most people around her in the present do not even suspect the extent of the pain and fear she often experiences.

The cumulative effects of these past traumas, combined with their fear-based emotions, now prevent her from moving forward in her present life. Fear can be crippling; it causes one to believe they cannot take risks, move into the unknown, accept changes, or endure unexpected shock. At the most primal level, the BodyMind equates these actions with loss, rejection, and abandonment. She has a strong need to know what the future holds, as well as a need to always feel in control of every situation. Because total control is never truly possible, her fear Patterns now cause her to feel immobilized, despite what her conscious mind and heart may want.

There are many other Patterns connected with this story in addition to the fear of personal rejection; however, this is the primary manner in which her fear manifests today. In that past life, she felt responsible for having contracted leprosy. She believed as the others, that this was a sign she deserved to be rejected by the gods, her family, and the whole tribe. She could not comprehend how she had "sinned," therefore she decided that it was her very being—who she was in and of herself—that was the underlying cause of her rejection. She felt this somehow provided a reason for the need to obliterate her very identity.

Today, she experiences deep, personal self-doubts, always feeling the need to compare her actions, values, and tastes against those of others. Whenever she feels even slightly different from those around her, she fears she might again become an outcast whose name is an anathema.

When one's painful experience involve a disfiguring disease, profound rejection, and a horrifying death, the body naturally seeks to avoid reexperiencing any of these by also avoiding its cause. Yet, in this situation, how does she know what to avoid? Because of the uncertainty, the body perceives the potential for rejection everywhere! She compensates for the pain this engenders through being highly accomplished in her work, doing only what pleases others, striving to overcome obstacles without seeking assistance, and, most especially, by becoming self-sufficient. All these are worthy achievements, yet they still coexist with and are based on the experiences of a frightened, rejected woman.

Rejection and personal achievement represent opposite poles on a continuum. That ancient lifetime, with its tremendous loss and rejection, was merely the beginning of her Soul's journey. She has reached a point of worldly attainment in this life because the events and emotions in that one compelled her to find personal acceptance in the world. Often, inside a powerful and successful businesswoman, lies an equally powerful memory of a poverty-stricken street person. Thus, in seeking to avoid being rejected again, she has used her fears as an impetus for her personal growth. And yet, to keep from triggering an unwanted effect, one will often reject the personal history that contains the cause.

Today her body holds dual rejection-avoidance reactions: the "Young Outcast" regards those in power to be like the leaders who ejected her from the village, while the "Accomplished One" rejects those who are sickly, weak, or dishonored. She is both identities, and everything in between. This means her body holds not only all the wisdom each identity has acquired, but also the accumulated wisdom attained throughout her Soul's journey. It was on this journey—from being totally rejected by her tribe in the past to being seen as a successful member of society today—

that she has gathered all the wisdom she now possesses. The pain she feels when she sees one who is physically handicapped, or another who is homeless, is the same pain her outcast-self felt in that lifetime. She will avoid noticing them by averting her gaze. She does not want to acknowledge that there are still outcasts within society, because she still retains these painful memories within the depths of her body. After she integrates all this, however, she will have great compassion for such persons, without being triggered into the horrendous fear and pain that they now engender in her.

When she begins to identify all the ways this story affects her beliefs, her choices, and indeed many aspects of her life, she will also uncover its many gifts as well. Her capacity for acceptance of others and her compassion for "the rejected" are boundless. Her ability to overcome adversity is also a powerfully earned gift. Other attributes still will make themselves known as many layers of fear are sloughed off by her willingness to work with the clearing energies. Thus will she find she possesses a capacity to heal that few can match. This gift of healing will appear in greater measure as she learns to lovingly accept all parts of herself unconditionally.

Transmission:
"Starvation and Weight Issues"

We have been attempting to teach about the formation of survival Patterns recorded in the DNA; however, additional body habit Patterns accumulated down through time are also outdated and call for readjustment. One is the excess accumulation of adipose tissue in the body, or obesity. There is a reason for this.

Throughout the history of life on this planet, starvation or lack of sufficient food has occurred so often that it is the rule instead of the exception. Those who truly had enough to eat were the very wealthy, and sometimes they suffered different maladies because of their overindulgence. Historically, the numbers of those "without" have always far exceeded the more privileged; hence, issues around having enough to eat are deeply conditioned into most bodies.

Given eons of human struggle to find enough food, especially in areas that suffer weather extremes, it is not hard to understand that the body's internal mechanism—the "intelligence" within every cell of the body—would create strategies to use whatever nourishment was available to keep the physical form from perishing due to lack. In the body, the food storage mechanism is second only to the heart-lung combination in sophistication. By this we mean, after air and blood, the body's assimilation of water and food is of the highest priority.

The body has developed strategies and "fall back" plans that are intricate and ubiquitously present in every cell. Unfortunately, there are times when the physical form fails to readjust its settings after no longer needing these strategies; hence, they may operate on "emergency mode" far longer than needed.

Those persons who have the greatest difficulty in maintaining normal body weight and distribution are actually those who also have the highest "survival intelligence quotient" as well. Often this is because they still carry a powerful genetic inheritance: their bodies hold ancestral memories of horrific loss or deprivation. Yet, the fact that they are alive in a physical body today is proof their ancestors lived through such conditions and then passed on to their descendants an internal mechanism focused on surviving any potential starvation.

Ironically, to eliminate excessive stored tissue, they are often placed on what the body may perceive to be starvation-level eating regimes. This only further refines the intricate mechanism and enhances the body's ability to do without. When they resume normal eating after a period of limited intake, their body becomes even more adept at storing the food against future "starvation." This becomes an often-repeated process, until the body simply becomes too exhausted to change its internal settings from "starvation" to "abundance" and back. It therefore begins to maintain the setting it believes will offer the greatest chance of survival.

Science has already proved that the cycle of severe dieting actually can lead to a lifetime of weight problems unless a lower-than-normal intake is maintained—which only "confirms" for the body that the world is still a place of lack despite, for many, the presence of abundant food. One must remember this is about the intelligence in the DNA of every cell. If that intelligence believes the body is "under attack" it will fight back with unbelievable determination. The rational mind or heart's desire are no match for the body's survival instincts.

What can one do when strict application of eating/dieting regimens only makes the problem worse? This is similar to having a fear Pattern that controls the life and resists any reasonable attempts at change. There must be another way, one that departs from the old "strength of will" practices, which are merely one form of determination warring against an even stronger one.

Earlier, we focused on Patterns arising from traumatic events versus Patterns-as-conditions. Where there were emotional or health problems, we looked behind the Causal Moment for the decision, vow, or belief causing the problem. This condition, however, is not "behind" a survival fear; it connects with survival more immediately. A fear of not being accepted for one's religious beliefs may lead one to being ostracized and even persecuted, yet the belief is not life-threatening in and of itself. It needs actions undertaken by others *in reaction to* the belief to make it threatening. Without food and water, however, the body cannot live for more than a few weeks.

Generally, clearing fear Patterns involves acknowledging that the body had a valid survival reason for recording—and acting upon—its past experiences. One then learns that by integrating the wisdom old beliefs in the body can be changed.

It is the same in this situation—the body has a valid reason for the manner in which it takes in and assimilates food; that reason is based on millennia of real experiences around lack and deprivation. Honor the body's attempts to survive by having compassion for it. Understand that, while the body might have been overzealous in attempting to prevent starvation, it is possible for it to be reprogrammed—not by further starvation, but by willingness to accept it and then guide it to another way.

Those who suffer with this condition may do so in seeming silence, yet they are rarely silent in their personal self-recrimination. Their internal thoughts are never far frothe struggle, pain, and self-judgments about weight. The key to changing the body's internal settings and resolving the physical condition lies in addressing these negative self-judgments. Instead of berating oneself for "being out of control" or for being an undesirable weight or size, one must be willing to develop self-acceptance.

It might help when one realizes for themselves that this condition arises from the body's primal need to survive (which is self-love) and out of a love for life itself. This realization will halt the never-ending cycle of internal self-recriminations by replacing judgment with an awareness of Love.

Next, accept that the body has been overly successful in its zealous attempt to keep itself alive; this realization will lead to understanding and compassion. Finally, the body, knowing it is no longer rejected because of its weight or size, will begin to cooperate and no longer fight against the new.

While this process may take some time, one will begin to experience definite results if one consistently applies understanding, compassion, and self-acceptance. In the beginning, one may have to consciously note and then stop their automatic self-criticism every five minutes, then every half-hour, and later, once or twice a day until the habit is broken. A moment will come when the body begins to awaken more consciously in itself to the new realizations and joins in the process; at that point change will be effortless and the results will be lifelong. As the body learns it is accepted and *safe*, it will then reach a state of peace and normalcy. Replacing self-judgment with understanding, compassion, and acceptance creates a new message and the body is then more open to alignment with the present wishes of the mind and heart.

The Power Matrix

*A*fter our basic needs have been taken care of, we are able to expand beyond the mere struggle to survive. No longer wanting to feel at the mercy of Nature and outside circumstances, we seek to achieve some level of power over them. Power issues are therefore the thrust of this Matrix and the Archetypes associated with it are the Warrior/ Soldier and the King/Queen.

Among the Warrior issues addressed in the Master Alignment Program are the need to hold their post, to follow orders without question, to be in constant vigilance, and, most especially, what we call the "Horror Pattern." This fear Pattern is not exclusive to the Warrior, however. Anyone who has ever been exposed to something horrifying—and, in order to survive with their sanity intact, closeted the memory away—may carry the impact of the Horror Pattern.

This Pattern eventually creates confusion between the horrifying *event* and the personal *identity*. Those who hold this Pattern fear it is *they* who are the horror, and this belief closes them off from intimacy, as well as leaving them with severe, unexplained self-judgments. This confusion must be rectified before they are free to use their power effectively.

All male bodies carry DNA memories of the battlefield, either as a Warrior or as a Soldier. There is a major difference between these Identities: the Warrior is a natural combatant and will often seek out a military career, while the Soldier is conscripted to fight.

Generally the Soldier will find greater connection with another Archetype, such as Scholar/Teacher, Artist, or Priest.

This distinction is important for those who know or are related to Vietnam veterans. The majority of those who served in Vietnam did so as "Soldiers," under orders from the "Warriors," who saw the war as a way to personal advancement in power and rank. The two did not understand each other, especially because the Soldiers of Vietnam had a major "disadvantage": as a group they had evolved to a point where their hearts were more open than at any other time in history. This violates the first rule of survival in war: the need to keep their hearts closed.

On the battlefield, closing the heart is needed to block both the continual pain of having left loved ones behind and the devastation of losing their comrades-in-arms. In fighting with an open heart, the Warrior or Soldier risks seeing in his enemy a resemblance to a friend, and—in that one moment of hesitation—being killed. For those connected to the Warrior/Soldier Archetype—whether they have ever donned a uniform or picked up a weapon—this once lifesaving need to close their heart sits within their body today, closing them off from the ability to share the Love that is there.

Power and/or Love—an age-old paradox for the Warrior/ Soldier.

Transmission: "Polarities of Power"

This Transmission, received on behalf of a ranch operator in the North-west, answers the question of whether there are any female Warriors. It also provides greater clarity on the true use of Power.

This one has had many lifetimes in the role of Warrior—at times in a male body and at others as a female. In this life she is again a woman, and she is still a Warrior. The Warrior's spiritual role is "to cut through the darkness of the lie with the Sword of Truth." One attains this level only after many lifetimes of overcoming the enemy on actual battlefields, as she has done. Although she gained certain Soul qualities that have enhanced her character, today she feels blocked from achieving worldly success, and wonders why.

Several outdated beliefs imprinted in her DNA prevent her from freely acting in the present. Specifically, her body holds certain issues around the use of power. We must examine these issues from both masculine and feminine perspectives. On the masculine side she learned to exert power primarily by use of force—this is called "active power." In many other lifetimes as a non-Warrior female, however, she was the victim of others' misuse of power; yet, this still taught her how to use more passive forms of power.

Today, one of her beliefs is that only males can hold active power, while the female is always limited to using passive power. By active power we mean direct challenges, competition, and confrontations. We define passive power as manipulation, or what is termed "passive aggression." She is highly skilled in using either of these extremes on the power continuum.

Because she has experience using both forms of power, she is aware of their benefits and their drawbacks, yet this has only contributed to her confusion about *true use of power*. These past experiences created her body's "truths," which prevent her from knowing what is real in the present moment.

In her lives as a female Warrior, for example, she still drew heavily on her masculine side. Then, as now, despite being a female, she judged all feminine qualities and traits as "weak." Today she deeply resents being in a female body; she also feels resentment against males, because she sees them as holding all the "real" power. She is partially unconscious of these ancient beliefs, because at another level she knows herself to be a powerful woman in the present.

There are several other Pattern beliefs that her BodyMind holds around power:

- the insatiable need to see herself, and be perceived by others as "powerful enough;"
- the fear someone else can and will take her power away, or prove her to be powerless;
- the need to deny true power can exist in a woman, or in anything that relates to the feminine; and
- the need to "do battle" with men or the masculine aspects within others, such as authority figures.

She easily can find a reason to do battle—using either active or passive power—when a situation triggers her Pattern. Her body truly believes that she must have "power over" or else another must hold "power over" her, thereby rendering her powerless. As a Warrior, she has a natural aversion to being powerless, because, on the battlefield, this automatically meant death. Although she is driven by the need to be the one holding power over, if she senses she is the weaker one in a particular situation, she merely becomes passive aggressive and is then able to "defeat" a stronger opponent.

The information in these Patterns must be reexamined and, in some instances, revised or removed before she is free to operate from a more authentic place of true personal power.

Her Pattern demands that constantly, and with great vigilance, she hold an offensive posture. Because of this, she is physically exhausted—her adrenals are depleted and additional stress-related problems are beginning to manifest in her body. Staying in a state of high alert causes her body to remain in "attack" mode, which also threatens the health of her immune system. When feeling weak, the body valiantly strives to mobilize itself, sometimes beyond its available resources, for fear that she is vulnerable to attack. It is a vicious cycle—a fear of being weak triggers a high state of alert in her body and her response to this causes her to become even weaker.

In certain past lives she suffered defeat by others who were stronger. In this present life, especially in childhood, she has also experienced what seemed to her like "defeat" at the hands of her parents, teachers, and others in positions of authority. She resented not only their level of power over her, but also being required to do as they directed. She longed to grow up quickly so she could begin wielding power over others, believing that being the one in control also made her safe.

She is presently at an impasse in her life—a state that her body interprets as not being "powerful enough" to accomplish her goals. This only escalates her feelings of frustration and resentment. To break through the impasse, we must use both information and energy to help her clear the body's DNA of these long-held, outdated beliefs. We ask her to work *with us* by again taking up the sword; however, this time it is the Sword of Truth and Light, not a weapon of war. This Sword is used to destroy "the lie," which is her Pattern—with all its implications and permutations—of believing that she must hold power over others or else she is powerless.

First, we offer her a new understanding: a new definition of the word "Power." In the past, one's very survival called for attaining power over one's environment as well as one's enemies. That goal was valid at a certain phase within human development, yet it is no longer applicable *in the same way* today. One need not operate exclusively from the position of "power over" to survive. Instead, a more evolved understanding states that true power lies in having "power to"—as in power to succeed, power to express, power to allow (including allowing others to be powerful without seeing this as a threat to one's own power).

By owning all aspects of her power to, she will no longer see the constant need to operate from active or passive aggression to prevent an attack. One's power over can always be taken away by someone who is more powerful; while power to resides within a person and is less vulnerable to a lethal attack. Although others may be capable of preventing its expression for a time, power to can never fully be obliterated in the same way that power over can. As long as her body believes she has only two choices—to hold power over, or to be seen as powerless—she will always feel threatened, and—as a Warrior—she must valiantly defend against this at every turn. Thus, battles will ensue and she will continue to find her body becoming weaker in the process. Redefining true power as power to eliminates all need for vigilance, fear, and attack.

We would close this portion by stating that we honor her Warrior energy. We do not seek to remove any positive abilities she acquired in her Warrior experiences, only those that are outdated and bespeak of the fear that she must constantly battle to have power over; that she must resent other's attainments, seeing in this a depletion of her power. These are old survival beliefs that only keep her from being free to own true personal power. Being strong and powerful in oneself does not require that another surrender; true power and strength can accept power in oneself while simultaneously allowing it in everyone else. Neither does the Divine call for the Soul to surrender (a word that no Warrior can countenance). Instead, the Divine seeks to have the Soul attain true power in order that there may be alignment of the One.

Question: "Am I doing what I am supposed to be doing?"

This is the Warrior seeking "orders" to act upon. When one has history of being a Warrior, there is also the habit of waiting to receive orders for each step, or else there is too much uncertainty in their direction. One's personal Guides generally do not interfere unless there is a need to give a warning. Given free will, it is not appropriate for anyone's Guides to direct each moment of the life. Always assume you are in the right place, doing what you are to be doing, unless there are internal promptings indicating it is necessary to change directions.

One always has the power to choose the lessons one wants to experience; there are no bad choices, only "hard" lessons and "easier" ones. Which lessons might be those that also rate the most "credit"? And which lessons might a Warrior be most likely to choose, given their nature and history?

What, then, is the question-behind-the-question? If framed in Warrior language, this question is: "What is my Mission—my Soul's Purpose in this life?" Here, we must remind you of something we have stated many times: one's Soul Purpose cannot be done *by them* as individuals, it can only be done by the Soul itself *with and through them.*

Everyone's overall Soul Purpose is to be who they are—in this case, a Warrior. And remember that it is the Warrior's role to cut through the darkness of the lie with the Sword of Truth. In each moment that you live and act by that precept, you are fulfilling a major part of your higher purpose. Before your individualized Soul Purpose can come in, one's body must be free from those fear Patterns that will block its manifestation. Therefore, your Soul's Purpose for you *in this moment* is to clear your Pattern around the use of power.

Why do I find difficulty in having enough money?

How did the Warrior get paid? Through looting and pillaging, yes? Your Pattern of the need to exercise power over others meant that to gain personal wealth you had to destroy them and take their hard-earned money. You were only able to see such situations in terms of win-lose. With the deeper wisdom of an Old Soul, you are now reluctant to gain wealth in this manner.

What you feel is really what we would call an "aversion." Because you believe that any personal gain on your part equates to another's devastating loss, you now choose to stay less prosperous, and then wonder why.

Remember, your Pattern holds that there are only two choices available to you: power over (which will also equate to wealth) or powerlessness (lack). Here is another way that your Pattern has brought you to an impasse. Clearing this by accepting true power as "power to" will allow you to attract abundance while recognizing it does not need to subtract from another's wealth or well-being.

Transmission: "The Warrior's Vigilance"

A nurse, who received his medical training while serving in the military, requested information on why he was having difficulty keeping his blood pressure in check despite following recommended medical procedures.

This body has accumulated certain experiences that equate any form of change with danger, suffering, and even loss of life. There is a belief that life is a battle, and that one must be vigilant against an unseen enemy who might approach from any direction, bringing death and destruction. Part of the Warrior's role is to provide protection, to guarantee the safety of all those around them. It is especially exhausting for the body when one remains "on alert" for lifetime after lifetime instead of mere weeks or months—there can never be rest, nor a period in which one might "stand down." This causes great stress on the body.

We also see within this body a vast abyss of hidden sadness, grief, guilt, and even despair. These emotions are masked by certain Warrior vows—decisions made long ago never again to be less than eternally vigilant, never to lay down one's arms, and always to be "at the ready." These decisions serve another purpose: as a form of self-punishment, a means of personal atonement for past lapses that caused harm to loved ones. In this, they also serve as a means of finding solace.

What then is the Causal Moment which so galvanized his body that it must hold itself ever ready to do battle in the present?

You fought in a war that raged for many years; it kept the soldiers at a distance from their homes and loved ones, though it was fought within your country's own borders. Always on the move, one never knew where the next battle would erupt, as the armies met and clashed again and again, season after season. There was little contact with one's family for—more often than not—messages would have to cross enemy lines. And these lines kept changing. No one knew who was winning or who was losing the war; all information was scarce.

There came a time, however, when the shifting army moved into territory that you recognized—those hills, that stream, they were familiar to you! Yes, you were near your own home and loved ones, and were drawing nearer with every step. Knowing this, you volunteered to scout ahead for the band. At first, the officers feared you would take the opportunity to desert, but after strong assurances on your part, they reluctantly agreed you might be able to obtain food for the group or discover valuable information about the enemy. And so you went, all the while knowing you would also find your loved ones to learn how they were faring and to let them know you were still alive.

Just as you were assigned to scout out information, so were there others scouting for the enemy. They already knew your troop's position yet had chosen not to attack because they were in unfamiliar territory and were also uncertain whether your band was alone or the leading edge of a much larger troop movement. They decided to wait and observe, while your own comrades also waited for you to bring back whatever you could. The enemy, noting your departure, sent a man to follow you, while continuing to spy on your ragged band.

You did, indeed, find your family; and the enemy scout observed your warm reunion. You could only stay a short while, barely sleeping that night to eat and visit with them. In your joy at seeing your loved ones again and because of your exhaustion, you did not know you were followed. The enemy scout was observing everything. He determined if you were welcome here, then these people must also be his enemy.

In the morning you reluctantly left to gather information before returning to your band. You promised the family you would see them in a few days when the larger group passed through. Tragically, after you left, the enemy scout used the opportunity of your absence to kill all your family. Instead of attempting to follow you, he quickly returned to his own army, reporting that he now had proof that this area "supported" the other side. The enemy leaders quickly made a decision—they attacked and killed your comrades and then withdrew in haste.

When you returned to your band, you found every man already dead—and you were devastated. You also felt in grave danger because you did not know whether the enemy was still nearby. You immediately raced back to your family's home and again found only death. All in a matter of a few hours, you had lost everything and everyone you loved! In the madness of overwhelming grief, you took full blame for all of this. "If only I hadn't..." were your constant words. "It was all my fault," were the others. Your family home had been destroyed, and everyone you loved with it. Your military comrades—also gone. You had lost another "family" and had no idea where other bands like your own might be.

Everywhere you looked, there was only death and devastation. You went mad with the sheer horror of it all. Yet, even in your madness, you clung to one thought: that this would never have happened if you had stayed "on duty." You began to mistakenly believe that if you had not volunteered to scout ahead, staying with the others, that your troop would not have been massacred. Surely, you thought, your family would not have died—you led the enemy straight to their door! You had gone "off duty" for a few hours, and it had cost you the whole world! You raged in grief and despair until, out of your mind with the pain of it all, you finally killed yourself.

We do not judge any of this, Dearest One, for we see only what you did for Love. Your madness in the face of their loss proves the depth of your love for your family and your comrades. However, believing that it was this same Love that caused all these deaths, your body still holds you totally at fault. You vowed never again to allow yourself to open to Love, to stay ever vigilant and on duty. Since those events, you have viewed countless situations as posing a choice between Love and Duty. In your grief and pain, you have always attempted to keep your vow—always choosing Duty, and never Love.

Your body has clearly equated Love with death. Based on this and other similar past experiences, your BodyMind believes that to choose Love only invites loss, devastation, and grief eternal. Yet, we point out an irony: choosing Duty is also about choosing Love. First, because this is a form of self-love; it is an attempt to preserve both your sanity and your life. Choosing Duty is also a way to save others from the deadly effects of your loving them. You choose Duty to save all those around you, for if you choose Love that would mean they must and will die as a result. *Because you love them* you must prevent this from happening, so you choose Duty to protect them—from your love!

There is another problem that arises from this, because at some level you fear that if you really knew you were choosing Love, it would drive you mad. The body, as we stated earlier, equates Love with death; therefore, if you allowed yourself to recognize the all-pervasiveness of Love, it would be the same as "seeing" again the total death and devastation that catapulted that young soldier into madness. If you could perceive that everything you choose is *always* Love, your body—because of its belief—would feel trapped, surrounded on all sides by devastation. This concept may be difficult to grasp with the mind because it is a nonverbal sensation in the body. It is repeating the soldier's claustrophobic experience of "everywhere I go there is only one thing (Death/Love)." Your body will feel panicked and look for a way to escape, as it did in that lifetime.

In these last few years, you have become more open to accepting new concepts and understandings—including the possibility of Love, Loving, and being Loved. Because your consciousness has also begun to grasp the eternal truth that Love is all there is, your body's past history with madness and its causes is being triggered. This is the true nature of the stress now experienced in your body. There is no other reason for this—and yet everything else also relates to it! Another irony.

Through this story we are attempting to bring light to the dark abyss of grief and guilt that sits like an abscess within you. We ask that you focus your compassion on your soldier-self; acknowledge the horror he experienced in that lifetime. In no way is he to be judged by you, neither was he ever judged by us. *Forgive him his innocence,* for that is what it was in truth. Realize that who and what you are today is a result of what happened to him in that lifetime. But for him you would not be the powerfully effective Warrior-Healer you have become today. Perhaps you will allow *your* body to be the instrument to release his long pent-up emotions. Feel his grief, his devastation, his guilt, and move it out as he was not capable of doing.

Be assured that you will not go mad, for *this* is your body's greatest fear. Indeed, your body fears madness—not death or mutilation—above all else; for if you have gone mad it must then mean all your other fears have also come to pass. Please forgive him, and then *you* will be the one who is released.

Transmission: "The Unseen Enemy"

Was it midlife crisis, the pressure of starting and running a highly successful computer software company, or past memories recorded in his DNA that was causing this executive so much stress?

This one has attained an age that in past centuries was often the limit of a male's life expectancy; this is one reason his body is beginning to experience fear for its very survival. The fear is not of the logical mind, yet it still strongly affects the various organic systems within his present body.

He is reacting to this survival fear by feeling anxiety, rage, and confusion, because he has no reasonable explanation for this sense of dread. This further awakens other impressions that make him feel as though he is sparring with an unseen enemy.

These are DNA memories of having once been a great ruler, one who led large armies into battle at the very height of his powers. His body, recognizing his present power and success, "reasons" that neighboring kings or warlords must even now be conspiring on his borders to take it all away, as they threatened to do in the past. His body is fully aware that riches attract not only others' envy, they also draw those who want to plunder it for themselves.

Therefore, his present age, combined with his worldly success, has triggered a Pattern recorded in the body's DNA long ago; it has remained dormant until now. For these reasons, his body has gone on "high alert"; it is becoming unnecessarily vigilant against the potential for an impending attack.

His body is interpreting some slight business setbacks as the beginning of a "campaign" that could lead to even greater losses. All this stress is draining his energy resources, causing even greater unease in his body, which also wonders if it is physically able to win the "battle." The body is beginning to exhibit physical indications of high stress, the same worry and concern he felt when, as the king, the "whole weight of the world" was on his shoulders. His body is doing what all bodies have done throughout history: it is merely attempting to ensure its survival. It is warning of a need to protect an entire "kingdom" from invading hordes, although he now no longer carries that level of responsibility. We can assure him neither he nor his business is in danger being overrun by an unseen enemy.

It will be very important for him to reeducate his body regarding its current location *in time*. He must also make his body aware of several other important realities: there is no vast "kingdom" vulnerable to attack; thousands of lives are no longer under his care and protection; no "approaching hordes" threaten all he has accumulated through his business success. He must use his quick mental reflexes to catch his body in its habit Pattern of wanting to sound a war alert. He can remind his body that, while its wisdom is respected, it does not need to experience such a high level of fear, because the present crisis does not call for "full battle alert."

We can assure him that in clearing this Pattern he will allow the possibility of even greater success and power to enter his life. It is as if he has reached a wall—a point beyond which he cannot go as long as his body believes that more money, success, and power will only attract even stronger "enemies." The body's old fears have stopped him, and his present intellect cannot explain why he feels deeply frustrated. Directly addressing these fears will break through the frustration, the anxiety, and the fear itself and give his body the ability to move forward into alignment with the present.

Another extremely effective technique would be for him to consciously forgive all those who in past lives threatened, attacked, and even destroyed his power. To continue to hold resentment for their actions, or to believe that the same could happen to him again, will keep the Pattern alive. It will also draw into his life the very events he seeks to prevent. Releasing all who may have harmed him in the past will free *him* from the fear, anxiety, and the need for vigilance, allowing him to pour all the energy previously tied up in his Patterns into building an even stronger future for himself and his loved ones.

We close by addressing him directly: Should you not clear this resentment, should you continue to retain it, it may turn and "feed" off you and your body. It can lead to greater physical deterioration, because its chemistry is harmful to the cells. You must use your natural ability to be magnanimous and apply this to your "enemy"; release him and all oaths of retribution that you have taken down through history. This will have the added benefit of allowing the Light to enter those places you perceive as "dark" within yourself, thus releasing you as well.

You have been, and still are, a King, a "Leader of Men." You have within yourself the ability to lead many into the Light and into freedom merely by doing so for yourself. You are able to lead, in true kingly fashion, through your example—by "going before" others while radiating the message of Light from every cell in your body, so that others may find a way out of the darkness.

Additional King/Queen Patterns

The King and Queen Archetype also represents the power of using one's personal will—"My word is law" proclaims this Archetype, which is associated with leadership roles. This Archetype's mission is to hold the Vision, which also applies to all true leaders. The King/Queen Archetype is also used to teach issues around personal Love.

For many reasons, those in powerful positions must hold themselves apart from those they lead. This creates issues around their ability to feel that they are loved for themselves instead of their wealth and position. There is no question the King and Queen know how to love "the people." That is a transpersonal type of love, however; while it gives them great sway with large groups, it often means they have also sacrificed their ability to experience a more personal Love. The movie *Elizabeth* is an excellent depiction of this Pattern.

Moreover, because those in the "royal set" were forced to marry for political or financial reasons, they may find it difficult to recognize "true" Love. So often denied the experience of personal Love, or betrayed by others who resented their wealth, position, or fame, they are never certain whom to trust. They set up tests— "If you love me, then you will know what I want." We describe this Pattern as "the insatiable need for Love on my own terms." As a "test" of their beloved, these terms are unspecified and therefore create potential failure—and additional "proof" that they are not loved.

Finally, since many marriages, and especially royal ones, were arranged unions, this Archetype may find it difficult to find a "perfect partner" today, because their BodyMind is still expecting the Matchmaker to provide one.

The Nurturing Matrix

The Nurturing Matrix encompasses issues around giving and receiving care. Some of the many occupations included in this Matrix are in the service industry, nurses, and homemakers—all roles we refer to as "Caretakers." This is primarily a female-oriented Matrix, yet there are many male Caretakers, just as there are female Warriors.

The Caretaker's most common Pattern is "the need to be needed." For this reason they seek to make themselves indispensable. Their motivation is rooted in the belief that their self-worth derives only from making others happy, even when it conflicts with or disallows their own needs and desires.

We must not confuse the *ability* to nurture and socialize, however, with the "need to" aspect that is always prevalent in fear Patterns. A new scientific study, conducted by UCLA and published in the May 2001 issue of the American Psychological Association's *Psychological Review,* found that, when under stress, females often respond by taking care of others—they "tend and befriend," instead of employing "fight or flight."

As we have learned working with our clients, a problem arises when Caretakers confuse caring for others with a belief that they must "carry them," a confusion that often leads to their inability to relinquish codependent behavior. As a result, Caretakers typically are physically tired, emotionally overburdened, and constantly worried about the welfare of friends and family.

Caretakers are often surprised to learn their Mission is simply "to care"—without the need "to carry." We couple that information with another teaching applicable to everyone: Changing every "but" to "and" will change your life. When approached to take on another service project in their already busy lives, if the Caretaker says, "Yes, I care about that issue, *but* I cannot do it right now," we have found that they begin to wonder whether they really do care. Instead, they can refuse by saying, "Yes, I care *and* it is not possible for me to do that." The word "but" nullifies the truth of any prior statement and creates circular thinking. "And" connects two truths, also making it easier to see the next step. We find this teaching to be a highly effective problem-solving tool.

Another major Pattern under the Nurturing Matrix is the need to prolong the state of grief. This Pattern is not exclusive to Caretakers; however, we place it under this Matrix because it generally relates to the loss of loved ones. We have seen this Pattern in an eight-year-old whose ancestor continuously mourned the loss of her husband for over three decades until her own death. Today, whenever the child is hurt, she is plunged into an emotional state far beyond what the situation warrants. Many women who have lost a child in a past life refuse to get pregnant in this one for fear their loss might be repeated; they know they cannot bear the depth of that pain again.

It is helpful for those with this Pattern to understand *why* they must cling to the grief now blocking their ability to fully live and love. It was explained to us as their way of holding onto their lost loved ones—by retaining the grief, they believed they could keep them present. The Caretaker, especially, finds it difficult to release grief, for fear that letting go means they no longer care. This Pattern ignores the truth that while our loved ones may no longer be physically present, it is our Love for them, rather than our grief, which creates the truer connection.

Transmission: "The Caretaker"

This woman, who is a spiritual teacher to many, had an unusual problem with her heart and was not certain of the true cause. Many other women may find the answer helpful to them as well.

The heart carries generations of recorded experiences around personal relationship issues. This is especially important for the female because of her conditioning throughout history. A woman's "identity titles" emphasize her relationship roles as wife, mother, daughter, sister, while the identity titles most often associated with men are those describing his business function in the world. This is so prevalent that some modern surnames are actually descriptions of ancestral occupations—Smith, Cooper, Baker, Farmer, and so on.

For millennia—indeed from the dawn of time—a woman's life revolved primarily around her family; sometimes her only value in the world derived from these relationships. Historically the female was taught to place more focus on the needs of others than on her own. When loved ones left home or died, she was then faced not only with grief over their loss, but also with a sense that part of her own identity had disappeared—the role of wife requires a husband, that of mother, a child. Therefore, both her personal identity as well as her value within the community were diminished when her relationships were gone.

Many relationship losses occurred suddenly, allowing her little or no time for preparation. This suddenness came as a great emotional shock to her body, especially after she had given so much time, effort, attention—and even her very being—to their nurturing. This left her with a great sense of bewilderment.

Lifetime after lifetime, one generation after another, all these painful experiences were recorded in both the DNA and within the heart center. Because her personal identity and worth were involved, it did not matter whether her relationships were pleasant; the intensity and shock of these losses were still imprinted in her body.

As the woman's body continued to record these emotions, certain physical pain and weaknesses began to appear in the heart itself. Sometimes this was the body simply using the metaphor of "heart break" to communicate its pain. At other times—especially where the combination of shock, grief, fear, and anger triggered chemical and physiological changes—the heart organ itself became weak. Heart symptoms might then reappear within the present life around the time of another significant loss; thus, if a beloved child prepares to leave home or her husband approaches a critical life-stage, the female's body might begin to signal a "high alert." (One such crisis period for the male body is between the ages of 56-60 years, when he compares his actual achievements in the world to his former dreams or personal vision of success.)

Today, female heart problems are often a replaying of intense shock, grief, and fear from the past. When it fears a major change within her relationships, the woman's body will bring forward physiological memories of prior recorded emotional crises. It does this primarily to remind her that she needs to prepare for inevitable loss. The body wants to avoid reexperiencing the prior shock, because it was the shock which often weakened the heart organ and made it—and her—more vulnerable.

Although a great number of women are more active in the world today, the female body continues to hold habit Patterns of identity, behavior, and self-worth based on millennia of past personal and hereditary experiences. Many women currently employed outside the home function as if their co-workers, clients, or employees are part of their extended family. This is a welcome addition to the business world as a whole, yet it also serves to reinforce a belief that the female's only value derives from the quality and duration of her relationships.

At times, a woman who suddenly becomes unemployed can experience debilitating effects similar to those that occur with the loss of a loved one. This is because the experience of the job loss triggered her accumulated chemical responses from prior losses; her body is responding in a manner beyond what the current situation warrants.

At the critical period of midlife, the body is warning that if she sees her value derived solely from what she gives to others, then both her identity and sense of self-worth will disappear when others are no longer there to receive what she has to offer. It is the body's *anticipation* of an important loss that will often trigger symptoms in the physical heart. To prevent such a reaction, it is important for all females to consider the following:

- An in-depth review of their current life situation is required to determine where changes in consciousness, understanding, or behavior are needed so that the body's protective wisdom is honored. This may involve reexamining her life's focus and acknowledging her own abilities, potentials, and gifts.

- This review will often require a reevaluation of her identity titles from those centering on her relationships to those encompassing more of her whole Being. Realizing, for example, that her identity can be expressed simply—yet profoundly—as "I AM" is very freeing; it does not make her importance dependent on the presence of another.

Everyone needs to be reminded that, while both their mental awareness and spiritual consciousness are more advanced today than in the past, the body's fear Patterns can overshadow these advances in their concern for primal survival issues.

All physical conditions have their wisdom to reveal. If that wisdom is discovered, acknowledged, and integrated, the need for the physical condition often disappears. We recommend that everyone learn from the body and honor its past experiences with Love and awareness.

Transmission: "Nurturing the Hungry Heart"

This Transmission addresses physical heart issues and emotional nurturing, albeit in a different context than the prior Transmission. This reading was done for a woman asking about valve problems.

The heart is truly the central organ within the physical body. All others have their own rightful place in the life and health of each person, yet the heart is the most important. As the New Testament states, "There is Faith, Hope, and Charity (Love), and the greatest of these is Charity." As we have stated at other times, the heart is the metaphor for the emotions, and indeed, it is the connection point for the "emotional body." As such it is at the center of all relationships, both positive and negative.

One may be in Nature, yet until they respond with and to Nature with feelings such as love, gratitude, and wonder, one does not truly connect to the Earth. In the same way, one may be *around* other persons, however, the connection to them must be through the heart and the emotional body if there is to be any benefit from the relationship.

The heart is the point where true energetic nurturing of the physical form is taken in, not through the stomach or digestive system. If the heart is not open to receive, then the whole body is in lack, despite the food one eats. This often explains why those with heart problems may also have issues with excess body weight; this does not so much *cause* heart problems as it is an indicator of them.

Lack of nurturance may also show itself as severe underweight if the body translates lack as starvation. In the first instance, failure to receive through the heart creates a "hunger" that the body translates as a greater need for food; the foods one craves are generally high in fats and sugar, because both temporarily ease the emotional pain. In the second example, the body "gives up" and stops expecting to receive, and the physical form is gaunt or weak. When the emotional body is truly nurtured through the heart, the physical body also feels satiated. Therefore, directly addressing the true hunger results in a natural shift in one's dietary cravings and physical appearance.

Water has always been a recognized symbol for emotions; therefore, when one establishes a "protective" Pattern of disallowing "flow," the body will also tend to retain fluids. This, too, is another symptom associated with heart problems. The excess water serves an additional purpose: it shields the body from the physical sensations arising from emotional pain, acting like added padding over a sensitive wound. Releasing the underlying cause of the pain—the belief that one is rejected, unlovable, unworthy or in any way lacking—will end the body's need for these forms of holding on or holding in.

In order for the heart and the emotional body to feel nurtured, there must be *both* a receiving of Love and a giving out or expression of Love. For the actual physical heart to operate normally, there must also be an intake and outflow of blood. The heart valve's function is to allow the blood to flow evenly into and out of this organ. The heart valves problems generally involve their being too tight or too loose. Tight valves cause constriction in normal flow and loose valves allows too much blood to seep through. In either instance, the circulatory system, as well as the heart organ itself, is negatively affected.

The true underlying cause of these valvular problems generally arises from lack of trust within one's relationships. Feelings of being betrayed, rejected, abandoned, or spurned can emotionally affect how one perceives both themselves and others. One becomes afraid to "release" or to "take in" at the heart, for fear others will reject what one offers or what one receives will lead to pain. To avoid this, one may make a strong decision to protect themselves from being hurt or rejected by others. The body "translates" this decision as an instruction to tighten up the flow of blood into the heart, resulting in constriction. Because this involves exertion that focuses an unnatural amount of energy in one small area, the heart valve may eventually become strained to a point where it is no longer able to "hold" the stricture. This results in weakness and allows seepage to occur. Making decisions that do not allow the valves to operate normally causes the loss of certain physical properties: elasticity, resilience, and the ability to open and close properly.

Clearly the physical and emotional bodies are attempting to protect themselves from the pain of rejection and loss. While this is based on certain "realities" experienced in this and other lifetimes, it causes one to be shut off from Nature and from others around them, and disallows the nurturing that will aid emotional healing. There is a fear in the body that if one "opens up," they will be vulnerable to even greater pain than that already experienced.

Because this is obviously a Pattern, one must be willing to release it to attain healing. The first step is to acknowledge and to "own" the reality of past rejection, betrayal, or abandonment that caused one to feel unloved. It is then important to forgive all others who might have acted toward them in this manner. To accomplish this, we again offer the prayer of the Master Jesus: "Father, forgive them for they know not what they do." This is the truth within every situation in which one experiences hurt by another. Because the ones causing the pain are not *inside* the body, mind, or psyche of those who experience rejection, they cannot know and understand the full impact of their words and actions; neither can the one who feels injured know and understand the reasons others acted as they did.

Finally, remember that modern medicine, in attempting to alleviate certain physical problems in the body, has often mistaken symptoms for cause, ignoring the psychological/spiritual origin at the root of many illnesses. In order to have true and lasting healing, there must be greater merging between medicine, mind, and Spirit.

The Knowledge Matrix

*T*he principal Archetype within the Knowledge Matrix is the Scholar/Teacher. Because this Matrix is committed to acquiring and communicating knowledge, it also relates to anyone who feels it their Mission "to get the word out." That fits many modern occupations, including authors, those in the news media, sales, and telecommunications field. One of this Matrice's major Patterns—the fear of public speaking—is an almost universal one. Other related Patterns include various issues around the ability to learn, know, and share information.

- A hundred years ago, a brilliant young monk, assigned to do research in the Vatican library, was also prohibited from examining certain texts. When, out of intellectual curiosity, he delved into the volumes and found they held incredible "discoveries" that could benefit thousands, his superiors admonished him, and he was ordered to forget all he learned. Greatly conflicted, he was so troubled that he ultimately went mad. Today, while testing in the genius range, he finds he has no stomach for research and refuses to apply himself academically.

- A medieval herbalist, labeled a witch and burned at the stake, today finds that neither she nor her work in alternative medicine is understood; thus she settles for an unfulfilling but less controversial career.

- An illiterate evangelist, mocked when he tried to preach the bible he could not read, died frustrated and disheartened when no one would listen to him despite his religious fervor. Although today he has a learning disability that hampers him, he is a teacher of teachers who drives his students, constantly demanding they work harder to make themselves understood.

- A Hawaiian Kahuna predicted the arrival of the white men and told his people to welcome them in great celebration, then died in horror and guilt as the sailors bludgeoned him and his beloved people to death. His last dying thoughts are "I should have known. I am responsible for all of this, because *I should have known.*" Today, as a female lawyer, she is too terrified to represent clients, fearing she can never know enough to adequately protect them.

- A student spent so many lifetimes as a Hebrew and Oriental scholar that today he carries the habit Pattern of trying to read from right to left instead of left to right.

- A Native American woman was nearly deaf, and thus while all the other women in the tribe gossiped as they worked, she seldom joined in, staying quietly introspective. The council of elders sought her counsel, and by the end of her life she was revered as the "Wise Woman" of the tribe. Today, her descendant often finds it difficult to engage in social small talk and judges herself to be inadequate as a communicator.

- A frontier teacher contractually agreed never to marry as a condition of her employment. She needed to remain chaste— or at the very least appear to be—in order to keep her job. Today she wonders why she is afraid to have a relationship.

Transmission: "Love of Knowledge"

In Canterbury Tales, *Chaucer describes perfectly the goal of this Matrix "Gladly would he learn, and gladly teach." When not able to do either, the Scholar/Teacher feels they have lost the right to BE.*

Beloved, we would address your Soul's longing for Itself, which is your desire to find your true identity in the present. You have long sought to gain wisdom and knowledge. Therefore you spent several lifetimes in the temple or convent, primarily because these were also centers for learning; they contained the libraries, classrooms, and others like yourself who hungered for intellectual truth and understanding. One with this goal expresses through the role of Scholar/Teacher, yet you feel blocked and desire greater understanding.

Through a myriad of experiences in your past lives you gained enormous wisdom, while also acquiring several fear Patterns that are now being triggered by your desire to again come forward as a Scholar/Teacher.

This Archetype has two aspects: the Scholar, who focuses on acquiring knowledge, and the Teacher, who has the obligation to disseminate it. Fear Patterns that were imprinted by your past experiences prevent you from freely living either side of this role. The principal fear that blocks you in the present is a belief that you are "inadequate" to learn or to teach.

Acquiring knowledge has always been so dear to your heart, yet many others on this earth plane have not been as interested in mental pursuits. There are those who focus on personal survival, on merely coping with the reality of their harsh living conditions. At another level, some seek power through fame or riches, while others attempt to attain it using force and manipulation. In the past, when you were around such persons, you often found they did not understand you or your needs. For example, if you were contemplating an idea and appeared to be lost in thought, they chided you for being lazy and "good for nothing." There were those lifetimes in which you were also persecuted or killed for expressing your truth.

For centuries, many viewed reading, writing, and learning for its own sake as frivolous activities; and this was especially true in those lifetimes when you were, as now, a female. Throughout history, women were denied the opportunity to acquire a basic education. Society considered the female as little more than property belonging to a father or husband. A woman's main function, beyond pleasing her master, was to bear children, who became unpaid laborers or populated the army. Even in those times when having an education was honored, some cultures believed women were incapable of deep thought, that they could not comprehend the intricacies of philosophy, mathematics or the sciences and, therefore, must be excluded from the halls of learning.

Because others denied you the opportunity to learn in the past, today you feel uncertain of your ability to competently acquire and then share knowledge with others. Occasionally, your Pattern will trigger negative judgments by others; this only gives further credence to your own self-doubts. Understand that these judgments arise because Patterns will repeat painful events until they are recognized and cleared. One's prior experiences actually create one's present view of reality. When past fears continue to arise in the present, this seems to prove their premises are still valid. One who was formerly judged to be incapable of learning *expects* to feel intellectually unworthy and have others see them in this way today. Thus, another layer of the Pattern is created. The same is true for other aspects of Pattern, because, by their free will, everyone creates their own reality through their beliefs and expectations.

The Scholar's portion of the fear Pattern holds that, to acquire sufficient knowledge, you must struggle internally with self-doubt and externally against hostile circumstances. These fears create blocks that manifest today as "learning disabilities" which hide your true intelligence. At times you experience difficulties with mental processing, with memory retention, and with both written and oral communication. While the information you attempt to share is of interest to others, both forms of expression take strenuous effort on your part—which you then attribute to your being "inadequate."

As a Scholar you also have a fear—disguised as respect—of teachers or those in positions of authority. You therefore tend to blindly accept what they say as being valid even if it conflicts with your personal mental and intuitive understanding. This is a conditioned belief from those times when you learned that no "humble student" could ever question the expertise of the Teacher. Today in your naivete you tend to be too trusting of what others promulgate as Truth, merely because your Pattern makes you see them as intellectually superior. Your overreliance on others comes from your belief that, because you are inadequate, they must be correct. This only confirms your Pattern.

On the Teacher side, your Pattern also contributes to the fear that you will never acquire "enough" credentials. Hence, you enroll in class after class, workshop after workshop, believing the next one will finally give you the sense of having acquired the authority that allows you to become a Teacher.

The word "credential" comes from the Latin word *credo*, meaning "I believe." Those who "need to" obtain more credentials are really seeking to be believed, to be looked upon as an authority by others. In this way one can feel that they are more acceptable to others and to the world at large. They think they can obtain this validation through classes, certificates, and diplomas. No piece of paper will ever be enough to fulfill this hunger, however, because this need is based on a fear and all fear Patterns are insatiable.

Please understand there is nothing wrong with wanting to be credible, yet there is a difference between aspiring to have credibility and the *need to* be seen as credible by others. This need is based on a fear which, if pursued, will only hinder your progress. Every class you take or each credential you obtain with the underlying motive that "this one will finally make me feel complete" only adds to the Pattern.

Imagine yourself for a moment before a classroom of students: with this Pattern, you would feel great trepidation if you could not comprehensively answer all questions, if someone challenged your "credentials," or if another more clever with words engaged you in debate. The body will seek to protect you from all these possibilities by not allowing you to come before such a group. Fearing that you would fail, your body "knows" you will be persecuted for your inadequacies; it must prevent this by signaling you through creating feelings of terror.

This fear is actually a very loving attempt by the body to protect you from harm—here, from professional disgrace or worse. Yet, if who you really are is a Scholar/Teacher and where you find your greatest happiness is through learning and teaching, these fears are blocking you from is your true personal fulfillment. How can you feel confident about yourself or your abilities, if at the very core you have no right to BE?

All these fears also affect your ability to have a close personal relationship. Your main Pattern—the fear of being inadequate—creates self-doubts about being lovable, for real Love can only exist between equals. It is impossible to have true partnership if one feels they are "less than" the other. When the message within the Pattern radiates outward from the BodyMind, it signals others to treat you as "unlovable" because that is how you define yourself through your fear of being inadequate. Your Pattern offers you another choice: to be in a relationship with someone you see as "less than" yourself; however, this also fails the requirement that a true relationship is among equals. By clearing this belief and accepting yourself as both worthy and lovable, you will then attract those who see and honor you in this way.

Your past experiences have imbued the body with a deep sense of unworthiness, especially as a Scholar/Teacher. The BodyMind is mired in this belief and contains ample proof imprinted in the DNA to make this its reality. We would have you fully realize, Dear One, that your fear of personal inadequacy is not the Truth, it is merely a fear Pattern. Yet, as we have shown, this is so strong that it prevents you from acting on your heart's desires. We ask you to look at small moments in your daily life: it is your greatest joy to acquire new information and then to share it, to give a friend a good book, to offer directions to strangers, or even merely to answer another's questions—all these activities are very fulfilling to you. When you perform any of them, you are living as Scholar/Teacher. One need not stand before a classroom or proclaim to be an expert in order to teach. Any level of learning and sharing knowledge suffices to satisfy this role.

Transmission: "Speaking One's Truth"

A client requested this Transmission after he was diagnosed with throat and tongue cancer. His willingness to work on the given Pattern's issues had a powerful, positive effect in assisting his healing.

In a prior lifetime as a Priest this one was accused of heresy, of teaching truths contrary to current Church doctrine. What he taught then were actually advanced understandings about the relationship between God and humanity. He taught about Love, mercy, and forgiveness, at a period when the emphasis within the Church was on controlling the masses by instilling fear of a wrathful God.

His superiors cited him several times, yet he refused to change his teachings. He was punished for this: first by excommunication, later with banishment, until, at last, he was put to death for his "sins." The nature of his death was horrifying and involved torture, removal of his tongue, and finally beheading. All the horror of these experiences was imprinted upon his body for purposes of future self-protection.

The information in the ego/body made him fear expressing his beliefs for many subsequent lifetimes. He feared being accused of speaking "heretically" and thus being banished, shunned, tortured, and killed. Those in positions of authority—especially other men— were instruments of repeatedly triggering his Pattern. Because of this, his body accumulated more "proof" that it is dangerous to speak his truth and that doing so could lead to loss of relationships, reputation, work, and even one's life. Today, the fear that any or all of these could happen keeps him unable to express himself in this life, because his body equates any expression with death.

His awareness of Love and forgiveness has now reawakened, and he again desires to spread these messages to others. However, merely contemplating the possibility of sharing these ideas also reminds his body of all the horror he experienced during the original Causal Moment. The body fears for its safety and urgently reminds him of what might happen should he undertake speaking out again.

This also involves the ego, for it wants to hold onto resentment against those who, in both the original instance and in subsequent lifetimes, silenced him through physical, emotional, or psychological threats. The ego always wants to nurture justification for its rage. It has convinced the body that this rage, which triggers a chemical outpouring from the adrenals, is an energy source; hence the body doubly embraces it.

Cancer is a condition involving a chemical and emotional overabundance of resentment. The ego/body is attempting to transfer all blame and guilt to others. When one is resentful, they strongly need another to feel guilty, as in, "Look what you have done to me." Resentment causes the body to create specific chemical combinations that promote the growth of cancer. To counter this and nullify these effects, there must be true forgiveness meted out to all whom one holds in resentment, whether remembered or not, from prior lives or in this one. Using the words of the Master Jesus, "Father, forgive them, for they know not what they do," is extremely powerful to counter the ego's need to blame others for any perceived harm.

In the past, those who condemned him were acting out of their limited understanding in that time. They truly believed the words he spoke were harmful to the people. They discerned that the masses were seldom motivated by gentleness and would not "change their sinful ways" unless they feared their behavior would provoke Divine retribution. To those in positions of authority, it appeared that this Priest's teachings were irresponsible and, further, that they would have a negative effect on the spiritual development of the masses. His superiors feared the people would "lose their souls" because of the weakness of the flesh combined with the evils of the world.

From the perspective of the present time, their responses to his "heretical" teaching seem extreme and vengeful, yet, given their level of understanding *for that time*, it can be argued that their motivations were of the highest order.

All the parties involved learned many lessons during their subsequent lifetimes in order to advance in wisdom and also to balance the karma generated by these events. It is therefore no longer appropriate to judge either side as being "wrong"; doing so would cause his ego/body to remain locked in the victim's rage and resentment.

To move beyond this, we request several things of him: first, release all those who condemned or punished him in the Causal Moment; release, through forgiveness, those who in subsequent lifetimes also brought judgment, condemnation, or punishment whenever he spoke his truth; and review his current abilities, gifts, and understandings as a way of acknowledging his growth in wisdom—which is a direct result of this incident. This includes his now having greater temperance in self-expression, allowing others their own beliefs, and cautiously assessing his opinions before speaking. He must embrace this wisdom without blame against self or others. Last, we request that he show willingness to eliminate all guilt, resentment, or rage against others.

We also ask him now to begin openly expressing his beliefs to friends, family members, and others. Taking the other steps without also acting in this new way will only reinforce the ego/body's belief that he lacks the freedom to speak his truth. If others question his views, beliefs, and opinions, there is no need to overreact. Allow the fact that others may ask questions because the information is new to them and they seek clarification. If, however, others try to dissuade him from expressing his truth, it is best to agree to disagree by acknowledging that each side has different views and then withdrawing. Today his life does not depend on convincing others that he is correct or that others are wrong.

To him we would add: Review and release all experiences from this life around having been prevented from expressing your truth. Review and release all those instances in which *you* wanted others to change *their* opinions and beliefs, or in which you stopped them from expressing out of fear that they, too, would be harmed for having contrary opinions. You have developed an intolerance for all those who speak without thinking or are incautious in their mode of expression, because this is what triggered the harm you experienced; therefore, in those who act this way you see your own "shadow self." Honor the whole of yourself without judgment. Most especially, express your *self* in everything you do and say, no longer fearing that it will lead to banishment or death.

We send you Light in the Name of the Most High, for your mantle of Priesthood is still and ever about you.

The Creativity Matrix

*T*he multifaceted Artist is the best representative of the Creativity Matrix. Artists live to express the Love that they are through their art, whether music, dance, theatre, or painting. If an Artist is neither understood nor allowed to express, it is as if they have ceased to exist, because, to the Artist, art IS their life.

Artists are always in the vanguard, leading society forward instead of recording its journey from behind; hence, their work and its message may not be accepted or valued until long after their death. This is the "Starving Artist," a Pattern existing to one degree or another in all Artists today. Fearing poverty, many will focus on having a "real job" while pursuing their artistic career on the side— believing this will last only until they are discovered. Unfortunately, due to the dynamics of Patterns, this fear often proves prophetic, and success continues to elude them despite their talent.

Today there are unrecognized Artists, stopped from expressing in the past, who now find their bodies will not allow them to risk rejection or loss in the present. Many were prevented from performing because of sociocultural taboos, such as the daughter of a prosperous banker who wanted to be an opera singer in an era when a stage or performing role was considered beneath her station. When her father stopped her singing lessons, removed the piano from the house and forced her to marry his chief teller, the singer, frustrated to the depths of her soul, went mad. In this life, she has resisted all internal urging to take up music, unconsciously fearing that some "authority figure" would again block her.

One Artist's female ancestor suffered from severe asthma at a time when medicine offered little help. The ancestor knew if she allowed herself the luxury of feeling or expressing any powerful emotions, an attack would result. Her descendant's body today unconsciously steels itself against feeling—or expressing—her passion, which severely hampers her artistic work and affects her personal relationships.

From a Transmission on Love

It is the nature of God/Love to extend and express, and this is done through the vehicle of Creation. Love and Creation are inseparable; one invariably leads to and flows from the other in a never-ending cycle. All that exists is an expression of Divine Love. All of Creation is united by a common element: the Love that equals Life. All-That-Is extends and expresses Itself within all-that-is, regardless of the countless and unique forms of that Creation. This is similar to music, which has many styles of expression. Yet, despite its differing sound, tempo, or tone, music is always recognized and accepted for what it is.

As there are many colors both dark and light, as there are many sounds both harsh and gentle, as there are many tastes from bitter to sweet, so are there myriad ways in which one may express and extend Love. Those who choose to create through acting are well aware that the greatest among them are those who play the darker roles. Actors vie to portray the villain, or the one who suffers and dies; this allows them to explore their own breadth and depth, thus creating a foundation upon which to build to the heights.

Transmission: "Standing in the Light"

A very talented singer, songwriter, and musician was troubled by stage fright, which interfered with her ability to reach the audience.

In many lifetimes this one was determined to bring the Lord's message to others although they were not yet open to receiving it. Her efforts were rewarded by personal rejection and worse. With great enthusiasm, she sought to have people experience the same joy and freedom she did by "joining with the Lord." Unfortunately, those she tried to enlighten were more worried about their next meal, or the health of a sick child.

Her Soul offered her a chance to grow in this life by presenting her with certain rather harsh lessons, not as a punishment but as an opportunity to gain a greater depth of experience and, with it, true compassion for the suffering of others. She accepted these lessons, because she, too, sought to achieve a better understanding of why others had so mistreated her and rejected her inspired message.

We wish her to understand that she has indeed fulfilled both goals. Through her experiences of early deprivation and of having a child with a life-threatening disease, she gained the depth and breadth of understanding her Soul desired, as well as the virtues of patience and long-suffering.

While she is now more spiritually advanced, her body still contains the effects of her prior mistreatment; today this manifests as debilitating fear whenever she wants to perform her beloved music for the public.

In her former lifetimes as a priestess, the temple provided all her daily living necessities. There was little worry over food, clothing, or shelter; hence, it was easy for her to dismiss the suffering of those who struggled or lived at bare subsistence levels. Many who saw the comparative ease of temple living rebelled. Some merely rejected religion and stopped worshiping a harsh deity who visited such misery upon them; others were more violent, sometimes even against the temple residents. Unfortunately, she was caught in this violence.

It was the combination of her childlike religious fervor, coupled with her *innocence* of how hard others had to work to survive, that made others resentful of her Light, her joy, and her message. First, they would simply ignore her, then they began to heap scorn and humiliation on her. When she persisted in still trying to reach them with her message, she was stoned to death. Her body recorded all these experiences as painful reminders; it urges her to avoid activities that might place her in potential harm.

In seeking to avoid injury, pain, and death, the body carefully extracts "lessons" from every possible aspect of an incident, sometimes then generalizing beyond the specific facts. Here, her body has determined that *any form* of public presentation can lead to scorn, derision, humiliation, and even death. Therefore, it tries to warn her every time she attempts to "stand in the Light"— including the spotlight—to share her message, i.e., perform. Her performance anxiety is the body's dire warning that emotional and physical harm will result.

We ask her first to recognize that in her former life, her actions— performed in innocence and with all good intention—caused the public to resent her. She was a young Soul, who had no wish to cause any hurt or pain, yet that is what happened. Next, she must forgive herself and all who injured her in this or other lifetimes. Patterns continue to attract similar events into one's present life; therefore, she has experienced various forms of rejection and attack. This happened because she had either inadvertently triggered their rage, or they did not understand her actions and intentions.

However, before her anxiety can be eliminated, there is a second fear Pattern that must be addressed and cleared: the fear of not being "good enough." This also contains a fear of rejection. The specific Pattern belief is best stated as "No matter *what* I do, it is never (good) enough." We perceive the audience does not believe this; because she does, however, the "proof" is always there—in small miscues or wrong notes, for example. Looking for mistakes will not only confirm the validity of this Pattern belief, it will also add to it.

All Artists seek to express the Love that they are through their particular form of art—for her this is through music. Therefore, we offer the following suggestion: In her onstage introduction, it would help if she would acknowledge to the audience that she is singing because it is her greatest joy to express Love through music. Add to this that she also loves them enough to allow them the freedom to not listen (she can say this in a light manner to show that she will not force them to accept her "message"). She will not need to do this very long, yet this simple technique will help her physical body relax, causing an immediate drop in her fear level.

We have suggested to other performers, as they walk out on stage, they take a moment to look at the audience and silently say, "I love you." Everyone in the audience will receive this message telepathically; soon she will begin to "hear" their response as it embraces her—"And we love you, too." Where there is the conscious awareness of Love, there is no fear.

Transmission: "To Voice the Love"

In session after session, we saw women who were not allowed to be Artists because they were women, and men who were not allowed because they were men. This can create "gender confusion," as it did for this man, who works in the entertainment industry in California.

Beloved, we find in this body a recording of painful experiences from many different lifetimes having the same theme: the inability to express your true identity. For you are an Artist, and the Artist's Mission is to express the Love that they are. If they do not know themselves to be lovable or are thwarted in their self-expression, it is as if the Artist has ceased to exist. There are two lifetimes that encapsulate how this Pattern was established.

In one life you lived as a young male in a small village. You desired with all your heart to be a singer, to express the beauty that you saw all about you through lifting your voice in song. Your father, upon learning what you intended, stopped you. A powerful Warrior, he questioned how you could ever be a mere singer. He berated and shamed you, ridiculing your sexuality. He proclaimed that it was not right for any man to focus on singing as a career. He sent you off to war, believing that by becoming a soldier this would "make a man out of you."

We must explain that there is a difference between a true Warrior like your father, for whom aggression comes naturally, and a soldier, who is conscripted to fight. As an Artist, you do not have a Warrior's nature; thus, your father tried to force you into becoming something you were not.

Artists are naturally sensitive at all levels of their being, absorbing sensations not only through the five senses, but also through the very pores of their skin. Artists see, hear, and sense what others cannot perceive. Therefore, being forced to experience the horrors of the battlefield caused you to become nearly crazed. The sights, sounds, smells, and terrors were excruciating to your body. The bombardments, the beating of the drums, and the cries of the dying assailed your ears. Because you were an Artist who expressed through sound, the screams—combined with the cacophony all about the battlefield—drove you to the point of madness.

Your father refused to see the truth of your identity. His Warrior mentality could not accept the fact his son was different than himself. In his mind, a man who was an Artist was effeminate. At some level he also feared that your choice reflected on his own masculinity in the eyes of others. Your father decided to make you like him, however, he only succeeded in losing his son, because you never recovered from the battlefield horrors.

Beyond providing for and protecting their offspring, fathers help their children gain a sense of personal identity. Too often they merely give the child their surname, and sometimes not even that. By your father rejecting you as an Artist and forcing you to be a soldier, you found your true identity destroyed, and this sense of loss persists within you even up to the present.

We would move now to another lifetime wherein you entered the monastery. You wanted to find an acceptable way to use your voice in song. In that life, you again had a father who would not allow you to be a troubadour. You wisely decided to be a monk so you could sing in the abbey choir. In addition, as an Artist, you naturally felt very close to God Whom you perceived in the beauty within all creation. You longed to praise the Creator of this beauty through sacred hymns and chants. The youngest member of the choir, you sang with the voice of an angel.

Even in that life, however, you experienced devastation. In your youthful innocence, you did not realize there were other monks who did not have your level of spiritual fervor. A few were there to hide from the authorities, disguising themselves as virtuous when they were its opposite. It was one of these who, upon hearing your magnificent voice raised in song, was stirred to lust and sexually violated your body.

The depth of your purity and devotion was so great that this attack was almost a sacrilegious act. It was a defilement of more than your body; it was a defilement of your very spirit. At some level you understood that your singing had aroused the attacker; however, you mistakenly reasoned this made you responsible. Thus arose another issue imprinted in your body, for you absorbed the guilt for this tragedy as if it were rightfully yours instead of the perpetrator's.

We want you to know that no fault was ever assigned to you; that is why we must state emphatically, *we find nothing for which we must forgive you.* Your singing was the expression of the Love you felt for God and His creation. You did nothing to warrant the attack. You acted out of Love and to express your Love—what is there to forgive? And yet, the guilt from this trauma remains in your body today.

The pain of gender confusion in your present body comes from these lifetimes in which your father maligned you regarding your sexuality and your fellow monk abused you sexually. In addition, your BodyMind holds confusion around how this relates to your role as an Artist. Your body's intelligence reasons that to be an Artist in a male body will lead to either madness or physical attack.

Today there is a constant sense of terror that you carry beneath the surface of your conscious mind without knowing its cause. This is the terror from the battlefield and the terror of the young boy in the cloister. Even minor disruptions in your life can easily trigger intense fear because of this.

Dearest One, we also find that you feel a great sense of personal unworthiness. These traumatic events recorded in the body leave you feeling especially unworthy of Love. If you believe that you yourself are a defilement, how then can you ever feel worthy of Love? The effect of this belief ripples out—you are totally unaware of your right to have your needs met, to have love flood into you from others or from the higher realms, to be comforted, and to have all these feed your heart.

There is no further need for you to carry any of this pain and confusion. Neither is there a need to see yourself as one who is worthy of abuse—this is not now and has never been who you are in Truth. Realize you are an Artist; you are one who expresses the Love that you are. If you allow your ego/body to proclaim that *who* you are is the opposite of Love, this invalidates your true being, leaving you with no identity and nothing to express.

And yet, Dearest One, out of all this horror comes a gift, for you have a great healing potential. Because of your prior experiences, your body still holds within it the poor, desecrated child. After you have worked to clear the body of these past traumas, you will heal this child by teaching him he is innocent of all wrongdoing. As you clear these Patterns, greater Light enters the place where there had been fear, pain, and guilt. The Light as well as the wisdom that remains from these experiences are all you need to send healing energies to the children you meet. Therefore, you will have the ability to heal other "desecrated children" by your mere presence—without words or techniques. Thus, what has been your greatest wound will now become your powerful healing gift.

The Spiritual Matrix

*T*he Priest and Priestess Archetypes represent this Matrix: those who gathered experiences in the ancient temple, medieval monastery, or as a Hawaiian Kahuna, an Indian Shaman, or in hundreds of other spiritual roles. One can recognize a Priest/Priestess by the candles, incense, and sacred objects they tend to accumulate on their home "altars."

Most persons consciously working on their spiritual development will have at least one of the issues associated with the Archetype. Their major Pattern—the need to hold oneself apart from the world—is covered in the following Transmission. This issue is critical because it interferes with the primary Mission of all Priests/Priestesses, which is "to heal the separation between the secular and the Sacred." Some harbor a secret fear that because they find themselves in the business world, it means they have somehow "flunked temple." Their need to escape the world also mirrors itself in an inability to stay in the body, which is judged as "evil" or "impure."

Another Pattern is a fear of being rejected for being imperfect. In sessions with clients who were HIV positive, a common experience has emerged: having failed—or been wrongly told that they had failed—a spiritual initiation. The aspirant was then summarily cast out of the temple and stigmatized as being "beneath the dogs on the street," not to be fed, sheltered, or even spoken to. This horrendous experience left a powerful message in the body, which still lives this rejection through attacking its own cells.

Transmission: "Healing the Separation"

We acknowledge her quest to reach Spiritual At-One-Ment. She has held to this singular vision since her earlier experiences as a Priestess. These spiritually saturated lifetimes in the temple contrast to other lives, when she struggled to pursue spiritual goals while remaining in the secular world. Therefore, she now equates living "in the world" with being kept from true holiness, because her ego/body believes that she can reach this goal only by remaining within the Sanctuary.

Today she and many other former Priestesses come forward with the renewed desire to work with spiritual energies. A difficulty arises, however, when they begin to realize they must work in the secular world; their ego/body seeks to keep them apart from it.

For some, their BodyMind remembers the masses were not allowed to look upon the Priestesses. To do so was considered a "desecration of the Temple," which they, as its consecrated members, represented. Yet we continue to ask all these former Priestesses to no longer hide their spiritual Light from those around them. We implore them to come out from behind their walls, built of these old beliefs, to share their Light, their spiritual teachings, and healing abilities with those in the secular world.

If she so chooses, becoming a healer is a way for her to accomplish this, as long as she understands that this will also require her to work with the public. Priestesses want to receive spiritual attunements because this reminds them of their former Initiations; however, they often shy away from using the energies to benefit others. They do not realize that asking for and receiving the energetic attunements without using them in this way sets up karmic indebtedness. Many who seek to advance spiritually do not fully understand this; they try to avoid public contact and revel in feeding their personal inner life by prayer, contemplation, and study, without then turning around and sharing the fruits of their efforts with those in the world. In the present, this avoidance is selfish and no longer acceptable.

This is only one of several reasons we request former Priests and Priestesses interact with the public. Another is that they are healed as they assist others to be healed. By teaching forgiveness, they accomplish forgiveness for themselves, which also enhances their own progress.

Reluctance to work with the public is a form of ego, especially in all Priestesses, who were conditioned to believe they must keep themselves "pure" by avoiding the "uninitiated." Inherent within such a belief is a powerful judgment against all others who must live and work in the world. This is spiritual arrogance, and it will truly prevent one from moving into the higher levels they so much desire to achieve.

Because this is a transformative time in the world, we can no longer allow those who see themselves as "better than" the masses to continue to feed their egos in this manner. They will all be challenged to allow spiritual energy and information to move through them and into the world for the benefit of everyone— themselves, the public, and all Humanity.

We have stated previously that taking on a healer's role is only one way of answering a Soul Call; it must also be understood that another part of the Call is uniting with one's fellow sisters and brothers in order that all—not merely the Priest/Priestess—may be uplifted into Oneness.

Therefore, we ask her to eliminate all ego blocks around this issue of the need to be separate. This means she must redefine herself—no longer seeing herself as one who is special and apart from the world, but as one who "brings the Light" to it by sharing her spiritual energy. Her ego/body will strongly challenge her on this point attempting to convince her that by working with the public she is "defiling the Temple." The ego will also argue she is becoming *less spiritual* by being in the world—we assure her that is the opposite of the truth.

We have often stated, "Many are called and yet *few choose*." The Master Jesus walked among the people, ate with the sinners, and seemingly broke many of the spiritual strictures of His day. He did not stay apart from the masses; He gathered them about Himself. He did not teach only to "the holy." Instead He came to release "sinners" from their misconceptions about themselves. Yet over the centuries His message has been replaced by the belief that spirituality required one to be "above and apart from" the body and the world.

Now is the time of Oneness. We therefore give a new directive to all who, because of their prior training, identify with the role of Priest/Priestess. Their Mission is to heal the separation between Secular and Sacred. Because the Priest/Priestesses are the ones who carry "the need to be separate" Pattern blocking their ability to advance spiritually, they must also be the ones to heal this by going among the people.

It might be helpful to some to remember that keeping oneself separate from humanity will also keep one apart from the One Who created humanity.

Transmission: "The Need for Perfection"

Perfection is an impossible state to reach on this plane, yet there are many who still seek to make it their goal. It is unattainable for several reasons, especially since there are no guidelines or standards by which perfection may be measured. In fact, to judge in any manner is to be *out* of a state of perfection, because this is of the ego/body, which is temporal, limited, and thus imperfect.

In any individual, the need to be perfect was most often established by conditioning in those lifetimes spent in the temple, convent, or monastery, where every moment was looked upon— by oneself and one's superiors—as to whether it was "holy," and thereby approaching perfection, or "sinful."

We would have all humans understand that, by origin and destiny, everyone is already perfect. This is because they were created by and of the Divine, Who is Perfection Itself. In their natural state they are Light-of-the-Light, for all-that-is can only be All-That-Is. Therefore, to seek what is already found is a fruitless venture, yet to truly experience oneself on this Earth plane is an adventure of discovery. One must live this adventure through all facets of "good" and "bad," or else the adventure is incomplete. Only the ego is blind to this; it wishes to impose its *own version* of creation—of "perfection" and "sinfulness."

The ego's goal is to be "god" in place of the Divine All-That-Is. It accomplishes this in many contradictory ways, using judgment, enslavement, and separation as its primary tools. It may attempt to make one feel both superior and inferior to others at the same time, thus creating great confusion—a key sign of ego's interference in the life.

The ego's greatest fear is that it is not "special" and more important than others; therefore, it promotes separation from those it perceives as "inferior." In this way, the ego imposes its own blindness to hide the Truth, until everything is seen through the filter of judgment. However, to gain a sense of superiority, the ego applies its most powerful and insidious tool making one feel "unworthy" by using judgment or self-criticism. When one feels the pain this engenders, the ego then stands ready to bring "consolation" by showing how one has been "wronged" by another, who must now be attacked to assuage the injury.

Those who must find fault in others to feel better about themselves cannot succeed, because doing so only creates a vicious circle. By attacking others, one forgets this also reinforces the belief that they, too, are vulnerable to attack. Instead, by loving and accepting all others, one nourishes the belief that they, in turn, are lovable and acceptable. One must choose which is their reality— attack or Love and acceptance.

The ego's tactics not only enslave one to its convoluted "logic," they also seduce one from the *real goal* of gathering wisdom from their experiences. The Soul understands that through their experiences one may come to know Self, and in knowing Self, uncover the Truth that their essence is part of All-That-Is.

It is time for the "game" created by the ego to end. Many are already choosing to walk off the ego's playing field, and their number will be increasing exponentially in the days ahead. We speak of the coming changes not as a warning but in promise. Also remember that those who choose not to awaken until the last possible moment will be as acceptable to us as those who awakened earlier. Love, forgiveness, and acceptance of what is can only lead to Love, forgiveness, and acceptance by All-That-Is of all you are.

Transmission: "The Suffering Priest"

This Transmission addresses the need to suffer to be spiritual. It was received for a man afflicted with Tourette's Syndrome a condition that causes involuntary body tics and vocal exclamations.

Beloved, in many past incarnations you sought to deny yourself any form of physical pleasure, comfort, and joy as a means of disciplining the body in the name of Spirituality. In a lifetime as a Renunciate monk, for example, you were even denied basic sustenance; you also spent hours in prayer, meditation and in the practice of violent penance (such as self-flagellation) that was torturous to the body. You were constantly taught to believe that the body was "evil," an instrument of the Devil, and something to be abhorred.

We do not want you to dwell on the details of the physical pain you endured, for this would only reawaken in you additional memories—of which you carry enough even up to this very day. However, we ask you to understand these activities were not only condoned in those times, they were honored, because their goal was to foster greater spiritual awareness. Today we understand such acts, beliefs, and values are obsessive, extreme, and harmful to the body.

Your current physical health condition is a direct result of the brutal pain inflicted upon the body during your self-imposed penance. In those prior lifetimes, it was also imperative that one not express the pain one felt during this penance, because any reaction nullified your "sacred suffering." One could not allow themselves to utter a moan or shout, or even weep. Many times your body knew excruciating pain, yet your discipline was so great, your self-control so total, that no expression of it ever passed your lips. All manner of suffering, all denial of physical pleasure, was stoically borne without expression. Therefore, today there is an unconscious belief within the physical body, built up over several lifetimes, that to complain about pain or discomfort, or the opposite—to enjoy pleasure—is sinful and means that one is "unholy" in the eyes of God and man. This intense control created rigidity in the body in this lifetime. Today, expressions escape uncontrollably because it can no longer be held in check. Exclamations of desire or pain that were withheld in the past now spew forth and the body experiences racking, intense pain.

Bodies record and hold the memory of all they have ever learned and all that they have experienced; therefore, nothing is ever lost. The memories are stored in the nongenetic DNA and have greater or lesser energy "charges" on them depending on the importance of the experience. In those lives that we see presently affecting this body, the charge was intensified because neither pain nor the terrifying emotions were ever released through expression. In this life, your present body has reached a point at which it has lost the ability to restrain itself from spontaneous exclamations (as would normally happen in a moment of great pain). Today your many outbursts are actually spontaneous cries that went unexpressed during past experiences of torture.

For the sake of your physical body, mind, and Spirit, we recommend clearing this Pattern of the need to suffer to become spiritual. To accomplish this we offer the following steps:

Note with specificity your need to withhold expression of both pleasure and pain throughout this life, being especially aware of the great shame you feel because you are unable to control your spontaneous outbursts and involuntary body movements characteristic of this condition. Note the similarity between the force of your vocal outbursts and physical tics to the way a body would react if it were subjected to a sudden blow. Seeing these similarities will greatly assist the BodyMind in beginning the process of releasing your Pattern of the need to suffer.

Understand that the shame you feel arose from the belief that responding in any manner to spiritual discipline nullified the act of suffering. There is a corollary belief that you are worthy of additional punishment if you are unable to control spontaneous outcries or body responses to the pain. These combined beliefs have the effect of triggering feelings of personal shame in the present because your condition involves a similar lack of control.

Next, objectively view yourself and your former superiors with the realization that, due to the level of knowledge of that earlier time, you all believed in the need to achieve spiritual detachment from the body through physical deprivation and pain. From today's standpoint, some of your penances are clearly inhuman and are no longer practiced to such an extreme; yet from our timeless standpoint, we see only the underlying motive, which was to reach spiritual perfection. We do not focus on the harshness of the acts; hence, we see nothing to judge. However, we do request that you release both yourself and others from self-judgment by stating, "Father, forgive us, for we knew not what we did." This phrase is powerful beyond measure to bring true healing to the situation.

It will be important to apply this same forgiveness to those who, in this life, were instruments of your Pattern—those who may have brought you any form of pain. As we teach repeatedly: if the BodyMind holds information by which it defines the person, then everything must align with that information and become its "messengers." In this situation, the BodyMind equates goodness, spirituality, and personal growth with the need to deny pleasure, to experience suffering, and the inability to express when in pain.

Because these beliefs help to create one's present reality, they attract others—especially those in authority—who will evoke painful situations in which you cannot defend yourself (cry out). This not only affects the body, it also touches on everything that offers it comfort. Merely trying to become a "better person" will automatically trigger pain, because your ego/body's identity is attached to idea that suffering is required for your personal development. You also experience pain when you allow yourself any forms of physical pleasure, because all pleasure is deemed "sinful" within the strictures of your Pattern.

It is easy, therefore, to become confused, especially if you believe that your feelings of shame and rejection arise only because of your current medical condition. Instead, understand that shame is part of your ego/body's identity: it has judged you a failure, because you lack the ability to absorb pain in silence. Yet, the ego is glorified every time shame is experienced in this body. Do you see how the ego has created an impossible situation? It is doubly "fed" by your inability to stop the spontaneous cries and movements—for which you feel shame—as well as by your deliberate self-restraint.

In the past, one who sought to be spiritual punished the body for its human desires, and even for its very existence. Shame was not only a motivation for invoking additional punishment, it was also a sign of humility—and thus of greater spirituality. Today the body still carries these contradictory positions while it continues to attract situations that trigger physical pain and feelings of shame.

To stop this endless loop, you must make a new identity choice. This will need great vigilance on your part, however, because the ego/body will attempt to trick your conscious mind. If the ego/body identifies with shame (in order to be holy), then one must consciously and continually avoid every temptation to suffer or feel self-blame for wanting physical pleasure.

We will work with you to remove the body's accumulation of unexpressed pain that has spilled into the present time. We recommend you create a habit of gently stroking or patting the body whenever a spontaneous outcry or physical tic happens. This small gesture will serve as a symbolic means to instruct the body that it is no longer in the ancient temple. The body must become more aware that it is in the present time, and need not be subjected to physical deprivation or torture. This small gesture will also help the body learn it is fully accepted and even honored as a companion of Spirit. The body is not a pariah to be set aside or disciplined so that you can achieve holiness despite its existence. We would have you note, and note again, that holiness requires wholeness.

All who have ever been ordained as Priests have a profound purpose in this life: to assist in healing the vast separation between the Sacred and the secular—this includes the body and all the physical aspects of life. Because of your past training and consecrations, you are indeed a Priest; hence, your spiritual life is still of paramount importance to you today. Your body's experience of striving for spirituality through suffering, pain, deprivation, and silence are still your "reality" in this life. We ask you to work with us to change that reality to what is true: of your very nature you are already a spiritual being. Therefore, you do not need to strive to attain *what already is*. As all Priests and Priestesses, you have agreed to bring your spiritual essence into an earthly physical form to help humanity elevate the physical into the spiritual, not to deny the physical in order to attain the spiritual.

If, in the present, something happens to trigger shame, do not entertain this feeling; immediately recognize that it is an element of your old ego identity, one you no longer choose to keep. If *any form* of shame is present, so, too, is the outdated Pattern upon which it is based. In that moment of awareness, you can choose to work with us to remove this Pattern by stating, "I no longer need to experience physical or emotional pain to be spiritual. I AM already Spirit-in-body, and neither my body nor its seeking for pleasure nullifies my spirituality. I honor my body as my companion in true spirituality. I love and honor all aspects of Self, for through these aspects does God experience His Creation. I AM an instrument through which the Divine lives within the physical world, therefore, I AM Holy, I AM Whole, I AM One."

Transmission: "The Initiate"

A physician who had been tested for problem in his lymphatic system sought more understanding about the possible cause of this.

Just as there are organs remaining in the body, such as the appendix, that functioned during humankind's evolutionary past, so are there also systems that are not yet fully operational, because the body has not yet evolved to a point of being able to use them. The lymphatic system is little understood, for it is a "future" system as versus one that is presently operating. The lymphatics are latent, because their "time has not yet come."

The true purpose of the lymphatic system will not be appreciated until there is less density and greater Light within the physical form—until the vibration of the body has risen to a much higher level. This system will be the circulatory system for Light, much as the vascular system now functions to circulate blood. Because it is not yet fulfilling this purpose, the lymphatic system operates at a lower vibration, merely collecting "dross" while the body is still moving towards greater lightness.

The lymphatics, unlike the cardiovascular system, do not have an internal pump; therefore, they must have manual stimulation. In truth, their pump is outside the body. As the vibration of the body raises, there will be an increase in movement. The Light entering the body from higher dimensions will pulsate as it enters the body, creating the necessary pumping movement and allowing greater flow throughout the whole lymphatic system. Presently, most bodies do not yet have sufficient Light to allow this system to fulfill its primary role.

We have stated the arteries become congested with cholesterol because of one's inability to feel and express emotions. The heart is the physical and metaphorical center for the emotional body. Failing to fully acknowledge and express one's emotions causes coagulation in the vascular system. In the same manner, when one does not realize and outwardly express the Light of one's Being, there will be congestion and even blockage in the lymphatic system. What hides the Light is fear, self-doubt, and judgment. The bases for these forms of fear are multifaceted. Master Alignment works extensively with identifying and transmuting fears and their corresponding judgments imprinted in the body, to prepare humanity for its shift into *Homo Spiritus*.

The reason this process of clearing is so critical now is that humanity is beginning its massive evolutionary shift, one that will change the importance of certain organ systems within the body. The adrenals, which are presently the "focal operating system" for most bodies, will move into the background as the heart begins to take priority. When and as that happens, for those who are working on releasing their fears and judgments, the lymphatic system will also begin to operate at a new level, fulfilling its true purpose of circulating Light. Then the body will evolve to a point where this system and its true function are better understood.

Regarding the specific body of this man: We find that there is a great need in this one to "hold on." He has never consciously fully understood this issue. The origin of his need was established during past spiritual initiations. In many lifetimes, he trained in the Mystery Schools, always seeking to absorb higher velocities of Light into his body.

To gain a fully rounded understanding, he has also studied the "dark arts" and the uses of powerful energies. Formerly, it was understood that all true Masters had to "descend into Hell" as part of attaining their Divine Self; this was part of all Great

Initiations. Today modern psychology speaks of "owning one's dark side," while theology calls it the "dark night of the Soul." The combination of dark and Light creates the basic wholeness of being that is a prelude to Oneness with the Divine. No one who seeks their greatest heights can escape the requirement of also reaching into their hidden depths.

As a direct result of his experiences, we find some physical, emotional, and even spiritual "scarring" in this body. These scars also connect to Patterns held in the DNA that now manifest in a general weakness in his lymphatic system. The body carries too many memories of bounding between the intense highs and the lows, between the dark and the Light; therefore, it is exhausted.

Much like the Warrior's pride in his battle wounds, he carries "wounds" from the challenges and suffering he endured during various initiations. His ego mistakenly decided that these "scars" were the goal and must be honored for their own sake. He held onto the scars as a remembrance of the glory his ego felt was inherent within them. Thus, according to the ego, the scarring proved his attainment of the spiritual "heights." This belief, insofar as it is an attribute of the ego, now prevents his integrating the "dark and Light."

These scars do not represent true spiritual attainment any more than a Warrior's scars "prove" the ownership of courage and valor. While such virtues may indeed be present within the Warrior, they are not "conferred" by the scars. A coward is equally capable of carrying scars. In this same way, his scars, in and of themselves, do not confer Mastery as the ego would like him to believe. They are the byproduct of the journey, not the final destination. His pride in these scars is one of the issues affecting the lymphatic system of this body.

Returning to his Pattern of the need to hold on: Several times he nearly failed to pass some of the rigorous initiation tests, and to persevere in such moments, he repeated to himself, "Hold on, hold on." Then, after finally passing a particularly difficult or dark initiation, he vowed to remember what he had achieved. This added to his habit Pattern.

In his past lives, he understood the great importance of reaching the "darkness" within himself. He also understood that many who sought spiritual perfection lacked the courage and fortitude to "descend into Hell," as he had done repeatedly. He was not only proud of his achievements, he also chose to retain them in the forefront of his body's memory, partially because he hoped this would prevent him from repeating these trials at another time.

The body then became confused. His body misinterpreted this need, telling the lymphatic system to "hold onto" the Light, instead of allowing it to flow. Light cannot be static; by its very nature it must move. If the blood stops flowing in the body, the body dies. The "blood" of the LightBody is Light, and it must flow for it to be nourished.

When the body has collected, assimilated, and condensed many divergent lessons into one simple "formula"—here, the need to hold on—that formula gets applied universally throughout the life. He has then found great difficulty in making choices in his normal everyday circumstances, because his need to hold on does not allow change. In addition, the physical body itself will take such a formula and apply it to many of its own processes. This creates stagnation where there must be flow, blockage where there is to be opening, stopping where there is to be movement.

One must understand that all initiations are "doorways into"; they are not an end in themselves, as the ego/body encourages one to believe. Passing an initiation allows one to enter a new level; however, it is not the level itself. Hence, he remains in the doorway, ever seeking another initiation for its own sake, instead of realizing that this is not Mastery, it is merely the entry way into that level. He has repeatedly earned full passage through the doorway, yet he has not accepted that what is on the other side is the fullness of Life as he is meant to live it. The ego is too enamored of the "door" to allow him to move through it.

To heal this Pattern, we ask him to see that all is ONE. The initiation tests were designed to teach him that Dark-is-Light-is-Dark-is-Light; they are but two sides of the same thing. Yet, spirituality does not require unnecessary suffering. That is merely the darker side of joy—as tears are the other side of laughter. Spirituality does call for wholeness, which includes joy and sadness, "good" and "bad." Those who ask perfection from their human spiritual teachers, for example, do not allow them their wholeness and, therefore, cannot achieve it for themselves. Further, those who do not recognize and integrate these two sides lack the wholeness needed for Mastery.

There is much for him to reflect upon within these words. If he is willing, the whole is prepared and right before him, yet he must be ready to "let go" to become his God-Self.

Final Matrix: "Mastery"

Our goal is to become Masters of the human experience; Mastery is best represented by the Merlin Archetype. Merlin was the son of a King, the nurturing mentor and teacher of Arthur, as well as a Druid priest. According to some legends, he was also a musician and the engineer who designed and built Stonehenge. Merlin has mastered all the Archetypes and he stands at the pinnacle of the Individualistic Level, at a point that is a prelude to moving into the Transpersonal Level.

As stated earlier, there are fewer persons who have experienced this Matrix; therefore we have found only one major Pattern associated with the Merlin Archetype. Yet, it is still powerful enough to keep one from moving into the next level, because it prevents the alignment of the ego with the Higher Will.

To understand this Pattern, picture a forest village, where all the people work together in relative communal harmony. There is one man, however, who, unlike all the others, does not contribute to the hustle and bustle of daily routine that has made the village prosper. He is elderly though far from disabled, yet he does not appear to have a function or to serve in any capacity. The adults defer to him, always acknowledging his presence as he passes by. It is the youths who seem not to know why he is afforded such treatment; he does nothing while they have to labor. They resent the fact that he receives food from the garden, yet does not help with its cultivation. He is given a warm cloak in the winter but does not share in the gathering of the wool or in the weaving. He is clearly not one of the tribal rulers, although he sometimes visits with the elders before they go into council. Who is he? Of what good is he? they mutter.

Talking among themselves, they decide that because he does no work, yet benefits from the labor of others, it is unfair. And so, in their youthful arrogance, and without consulting their parents, they confront the old man, demanding he make some contribution, just as they must do.

His reaction surprises them. In an even, deep rumble he says, "Oh, so you don't think that I have a role within this village, do you? Well, let us see about that." And he quietly turns away.

In the morning there is no sign of the old man; his hut is empty and he has apparently left the village. The adults are mildly curious but not overly concerned, since they know he sometimes goes off into the hills alone. They do not know about the confrontation between the old man and the youths, who are strangely cocky that morning, acting as if they have a shared secret.

When the weeks pass and the old man does not return, there is a growing anxiety among the villagers. They murmur about the crops, and whether there will be enough game. Will the winter be a severe one, and when, oh when, is he going to return? The youths hear these questions and shake their heads. What has all that to do with the old man? Good riddance, they say, less work for us.

They did not understand that the old man was the Merlin and his role was to do as all Merlins had done before him: energetically support the growth and stability of the entire village. When Merlin left Camelot, what happened to the kingdom? The elders knew what the youths could not: that without the Merlin, they would face greater difficulties and more hardship, and possible disruption of the community.

Yet where is the Merlin Pattern? In getting upset over the youths' disrespect, the Merlin had allowed his pride to sway him. He left not merely to teach them an important lesson; he was giving in to ego. He was being challenged on his ability to get above the petty slights that all of us experience, without retaliating. In withdrawing his energies, he was thinking more of his hurt pride than of the good of the whole community. Even if there had been some level of justification, he was not to take it *personally*—which is what the ego encourages—not if he wants to move into Transpersonal living.

Today those who have this Pattern gain satisfaction from the thought that they are so important to their company/business/ partnership/school that when they leave, it will fall apart. This is an ego trick and a spiritual temptation. Those who harbor this belief will find they cannot take a vacation for fear their world will have collapsed behind them by the time they return. A belief that one is so valuable that they literally "hold up the world" is, in actuality, a crushing burden. Subtle? Yes, however, every Master must pass one last hurdle before they can move forward into the next level.

Transmission: "The Starborn"

This Archetype does not belong to any of the Matrices, because the Starborn is "not of this world." Yet this is an important Archetype, because there are now so many Starborns; they have a Mission to assist in (or merely observe) Humanity's evolutionary transformation.

You, Dearest One, are a Starborn, that is one who, although having a human body and born of Earthly parents, is not originally from the third-dimensional, material realm. While it is true that all humans are really Starborns, because they are in their essence spiritual beings temporarily living in a physical vehicle, we use the term to describe those who have little or no prior experience on the Earth plane.

Starborns have incarnated now to fulfill a unique Soul Mission: to assist humanity in its transition from *Homo sapiens* into *Homo Spiritus.* Hence, many have agreed to come here from another time or space dimension to teach or be examples for humanity. This requires them to take on a physical form so unlike their own Light Body; thus, Starborns tend to reject the body. Being unfamiliar with it, they fear the body's limitations will hamper their ability to perform their Mission. Their greatest fear arises from this: the belief that being incarnated means they will become enmeshed permanently in dense materiality and be unable to return to their own home.

Besides having discomfort with the physical form, Starborns also possess strong feelings of being isolated; they realize that the body closes them off from true connection with others. It seems to "cage" the mental processes, where before the Starborn was accustomed to group mind. While becoming embodied appeared to be so easy when they were still on their own nonphysical dimension, they now know it is not.

Because so many children born in the last decades are Starborns, we will first focus on the more general issue of having to live, work, and communicate while in a body. Incarnating in a physical form, which always holds archaic beliefs wrapped in survival fears, is very confusing to a highly developed Light Being. They begin to realize their body and mind are often at odds with one another. When Starborns first take on a physical form, unfamiliar feelings, emotions, unconscious beliefs, and behaviors can overwhelm them. If their prior experiences were in predominantly non-physical dimensions, they struggle daily to understand not only the "rules of the game," but also the swirling unreality of it all.

Although most of a Starborn's fear Patterns are not of their own creation—because they are biologically inherited—these fears are still very real to the BodyMind. Hence, Starborns may find themselves reacting in undesirable ways and must constantly contend with instinctual responses established by past ancestral choices and experiences.

It will help all Starborns immeasurably if they understand certain truths: that they are not native to this plane and manner of being; that they must live in a physical form imbued with millennia of genetic fear Patterns that overrule the higher rational processes at every turn; that they *volunteered* to take on both this earthly Mission and the physical body (no one "did this to them"); and that the sensations of being isolated, alone, different, and abandoned are common to all those who accept such a role. Few around them understand the Starborn's pain, because they are more native to Earth—or if not, have spent more lifetimes acclimating to it.

Besides experiencing many of these same fears, your particular body holds a major blocking Pattern of the inability to express. This Pattern is based on beliefs passed down through your biological inheritance.

On the female side, for example, your body holds the Vow of Silence, along with its fear of revealing the "secret." Your body also inherited heavy conditioning from past Warrior ancestors on your masculine side. Warriors are trained to never question orders, and this imprinted conditioning feeds your Pattern's fear. Because of this, your BodyMind overrules any inclination to challenge another's ideas, beliefs, and orders, despite your ability to see an error or potential for harm. You find it impossible to challenge what, from a more developed sensitivity, you see as uncivilized, harmful activity, especially if an authority figure initiates it. You also know from experience that if you were to speak in such situations, there would be an immediate reprisal, reconfirming that it is in your best interests to remain silent.

You may almost look on this life, this Mission, as an exciting adventure, for you have come to teach, to bring forward new information to help people attain greater consciousness. Yet you find yourself in a body that holds several blocking Patterns that may prevent your accomplishing the Mission: the need to be silent, the fear of revealing higher truths, the need to hold the secret. All these require you to keep from being seen and heard by others. You are a Teacher who must not teach, a Revealer who must not reveal, a Light that must remain hidden from sight. Such has been your dilemma and your burden, and this is in addition to the Starborn's resistance to being in the body; you have had to struggle against this to fulfill your goals. Yet we want you to know that you have not failed in your Mission.

Because some might find it difficult to assimilate the fact you are a Starborn, it is wise to withhold that information from others— not out of the need to be secretive, rather, in prudence. However, a time is coming when the existence of Starborns will be widely known and accepted. In addition, others will understand that

Starborns have come here for a higher purpose. As human consciousness expands, there will be widespread acknowledgment that other worlds and dimensions exist. This Earth will awaken to the understanding of Oneness—an idea you have lived and experienced in your own dimension. It is for that very reason you are here. Humanity needs those who are experts in the of Oneness to help in this time of transition.

Time is of the essence, for the transition is quickly approaching. We honor all who have chosen to come from other time and space dimensions to assist the Earth and the whole of humanity. We want you to understand you have neither been abandoned here nor are you marooned to physicality for all eternity. You have come for a specific purpose and have found living here difficult. We will aid in other ways, such as by creating a greater link to your own time/space dimension. This will ease your sense of aloneness and expand your ability to access both guidance and your higher dimensional "tool box."

You have sensed early that there were better means of accomplishing certain tasks on this planet, yet your Earthly awareness could not quite grasp the way to do this. For example, moving through time and space seems excruciatingly slow for all Starborns. As you address the issues we have mentioned, you will find a greater ability to manipulate time. This will allow you to move through space with more ease as well. Thus, you will do more in less time and with less drain on your resources.

You have come to help humanity raise its physical vibration so that it can begin to receive and use greater velocities of Light. As we work with you to transmute the fear Patterns, you will find your body will become less dense and better able to carry more Light, thus making it easier for you to work on the physical plane. Holding more Light in your body also will help you feel less alien here.

We ask you to be more accepting of the physical form, realizing that, although it may be cumbersome by your Light Body standards, taking on the body is an important part of your Mission. The body is comprised of the same elements as the Earth; hence, the body receives its energetic nurturing by maintaining a connection with her, much like a lamp receives energy because it is plugged into the power source. Staying grounded within your body allows the Earth to replenish it without causing you to become mired in physicality. Feel your connection to the Earth; she understands who you are in truth, and that you have come to assist her. She seeks to honor and nurture you for your role here, not hold you back.

Why do I have difficulty knowing and acting on my desires?

The main confusion revolves around your true identity as Starborn. You perceive what those on the Earthly dimension judge to be desirable and what they strive to attain, and you wonder why you seem to have different values. Often, those having a sense of not belonging (as you did, especially in your youth) will try to fit in by acting like others and attempting to emulate their values, even though these feel "alien."

You have difficulty knowing what you want because you have not known *who you are*. Your values, wants, and desires are beyond the level of this plane's understanding; hence, you sense an inarticulate longing for that which is not here. It is a yearning for the openness, wholeness, connectedness, and the Light of your true home, while you presently exist in a place of relative secrecy, separation, and darkness.

You wish to bring openness, wholeness, and connection to others by sharing information (which to you is Light), while the fear Patterns in your present physical body hold that these activities will cause you to be killed.

Realizing and accepting who you are will go a long way not only to explain the blocks you have experienced up to now, it will also help you move beyond them. Even if you never stand before a classroom, or an audience, you will teach everyone you meet through the Light of your very Being.

In addition, certain religious beliefs conditioned into your ancestors required that one bring the body into "submission." Therefore, if any of your "wants and desires" would offer comfort and joy to the physical body, this conditioning says that you must neither contemplate nor try to acquire them.

Realize that the Divine created everything on this plane for joy and upliftment. The true standard for judging one's desires is not whether they are "sinful"; rather it is the standard of "harmlessness": If what one desires does not harm the self or others, then it may be embraced in joyful thanksgiving to the Divine Father, Who is its Source.

We honor you and an untold number of other Starborns. You are aiding in the very evolutionary quantum leap that your own dimension experienced thousands of light years ago. It is indeed an exciting opportunity to be present at the creation of a new species. Remember that you are not, nor have you ever been, alone. You have come to teach and to demonstrate that no one is separate and alone—instead, we are ALL ONE.

Part Three:
Clearing Techniques

Introduction

*I*n Master Alignment, we use several techniques to clear fear Patterns from the body; the primary method is the BodyMind Alignment session. Here an individual's key Pattern is presented and discussed, and the Practitioner transmits fifth-dimensional energies that rewrite it at the DNA level, which is beyond mere "cellular memory." These energies stay with the person beyond the session, allowing them to clear other Patterns later. The Level I program, "Transmuting the DNA," also contains both information and energy to assist participants in clearing their more *generic* Patterns. However, this Program does not replace the personal session.

There is a possibility there will be energies benefiting those reading this book—exactly how or to what degree is yet unknown. The energy will be alongside or within the written words. Accepting this as a real possibility, we encourage all of you to study and apply the information in this section for the greatest effect.

Through articles and Transmissions, we will explore three major clearing processes: "Willingness, Awareness, and Choice"; "Refocusing to the Heart"; and "Choose Again." Simply knowing and recognizing a Pattern is not enough. It must first be rewritten in the DNA, and then its effects must be cleared from the cellular memory and from the unconscious. This is accomplished primarily through the Willingness, Awareness, and Choice process. Refocusing and Choose Again are advanced processes that are only effective if Willingness is also applied.

Willingness, Awareness, and Choice

*I*n the personal BodyMind Alignment session, the client is always trained in Willingness, Awareness, and Choice. While the Pattern imprinted in the DNA is rewritten by the energies, further clearing must be accomplished to make certain the Pattern is not validated and thus reprinted by one's beliefs and actions. This additional clearing removes all evidence of the Pattern not only from the DNA but also throughout the body.

The ongoing clearing process is critically important for another reason: We now understand it is training us in true use of our personal will. There is no academic course that prepares us to correctly exercise this powerful faculty, yet correct use of will allows us to become co-creators with the Divine; in short, it is *the* tool needed to accomplish miracles.

Because applying the Willingness, Awareness, and Choice process is so central to clearing the body, after discussing its basic elements, we will examine several excerpts from prior Transmissions to take a more thorough look at its many aspects.

The Basic Teaching

Many Transmissions reiterate that only Willingness is required to release our Patterns. On its face that may sound easy, until we learn that Willingness also means we must agree to release the rage and blame that so often lie concealed within every Pattern.

The Refocusing Transmission points out that one can easily become addicted to the chemicals that anger and resentment trigger in our bodies. (We were told some fibromyalgia is caused by an allergic reaction to these same chemicals; whenever they are released due to stress or anger, there is internal inflammation and pain.)

There is another problem that arises if the word "willingness" is defined as a desire to have the problem fixed—in this case, have the Pattern removed—while we remain passive: "Oh, I'm willing—heal me." This is the same as a patient asking the physician to cure their breathing problems while also refusing to give up smoking. They are *more than willing* to have the symptoms alleviated, without taking action to remove their cause.

Neither is Willingness "waiting to want to." It is an act of exercising one's personal will despite what the body is insisting. One can exercise Willingness "through clenched teeth," and it will still be powerfully effective. Neither are persistence nor determination required, although they are useful for consistent application of Willingness.

Then the question becomes how do we know when we are in true Willingness—what are we supposed to do? One exercises Willingness through its two aspects: Awareness and Choice. Awareness is simply recognizing when we are in a Pattern, as we discussed in Part One.

There are three levels to Choice: first, refusing to validate the Pattern beliefs by entertaining fear or other emotions; second, deliberately requesting to have the Pattern removed; and third, taking definitive steps to act in a new way. Because we operate in a "free will zone," it is imperative that we indicate our choice to have the Pattern removed each time we note its presence. When a Pattern arises, this is not a sign that we have failed in our previous attempts; it is simply *another* opportunity to remove *another* layer of it from the body. The following excerpts from various Transmissions discuss additional aspects of this important process:

.From "The Tribal Outcast" Transmission:

To clear these issues along with their corresponding emotions, and to reopen her life to progress, she must work diligently using Willingness, Awareness, and Choice. This process will allow her to again have control over her life.

In the days ahead, fears of survival, abandonment, rejection, and unworthiness will arise in her body. As these feelings come forward, she must first note whether something in the immediate instance has triggered her Pattern. She may also want to recognize how her body has taken this as proof that she will again become an outcast. The triggering event might be as small as someone seemingly ignoring her question. In the moment that she recognizes the fear, she must then connect it to her Pattern, and state (silently is fine) that she no longer chooses to believe that she is rejected, or that she is an Outcast.

Last, she must ask the Light Beings, who assist all in this process, to remove from her body more of the Pattern that still supports these emotions and beliefs. This will take time. At first, she may need to do this process several times in a single day; then later, several times a week, until what had accumulated in her body now no longer stops her life.

Another technique—similar to Willingness, Awareness, and Choice—that may help is to state, "I choose to retain all the wisdom in this Pattern and I release all feelings of pain, fear, anger, and guilt connected to it." Say this when becoming aware of the Pattern's emotional reaction. This works especially well on old memories that validate one's fears.

It takes application and persistence to clear the body. The first six weeks of applying this process will be very important, because that is the time it takes for the DNA to replicate itself.

The Pattern imprinted into the DNA becomes part of the blueprint that determines the chemical composition of various compounds in the body. As the body begins to become clear of the Pattern, the cells will also start eliminating the chemistry of fear, grief, despair, and anger that is attached to the Pattern. These emotions are part of the chemical "soup"—or cellular memory—in each cell. She must also begin to drink more water to flush these fear-based chemicals out of her system; this will prevent flu-like symptoms that result from the detoxification.

From "The Scholar/Teacher" Transmission:

This is the point when true Willingness must be used. However, waiting until one wants to make changes will not suffice to get past the ego; only a strong act of will—made in the face of ego's desire to hold onto rage and blame—will work.

One must practice Willingness, Awareness, and Choice with vigilance and consistency in order to fully develop the "muscle" of Higher Will. At every step one will be challenged by ego, who relishes feeding off the sense of helplessness that "victim" engenders. Yet, at every step, one will also be supported by their Soul, Guides, and Masters to assist them to move into true power.

The Soul does not ask the ego to surrender; instead, it asks that the ego and the lower will align with the Higher Will. The ego has a rightful place within the being, yet it cannot be in charge if one is to advance into one's Soul Purpose; otherwise the ego will appropriate the higher energies for its own ends.

From the Warrior's Transmission

Everyone wanting to remove fear Patterns from their body must give their free will assent allowing us to assist them in this process—moment by moment and day to day. One's prior efforts using other methods have already proven that one can proceed only so far alone; for despite even Herculean efforts, one's Patterns still persist in blocking the life.

All we ask of each person is Willingness, which is comprised of two aspects: Awareness and Choice. How one exhibits Willingness is as follows: in the days, weeks, and months ahead we will offer you many opportunities to clear this Pattern from your body by presenting it in everyday situations. A Warrior might find himself before an authority figure, for example, and sense his body "girding for battle" because he feels a "need to win." In that moment we ask him to become aware that his fear Pattern is present; it came up not because he truly needs to do battle, but because this presents another opportunity for him to clear it.

Simply becoming aware of the Pattern within the situation is not enough, however; one must also make a new choice, or else they will fall back into their prior behaviors and thereby reinforce their Pattern's beliefs. In the moment one recognizes that their fear Pattern is operating—or promptly after coming to that realization—they must consciously choose to no longer accept the old beliefs and then ask us to remove another part of the Pattern from the body. One cannot ask us to take away the fear, or other uncomfortable feelings connected to a Pattern, for that we will not do. Instead, we assure them that, in most cases, these feelings will dissipate if full Willingness is exercised.

This process needs to be repeated each time another aspect of any Pattern is offered for clearing—sometimes several times a day at first. While the energy and information within a personal session (or Transmission) will reprogram the Pattern in the DNA itself, it is only through continued efforts in applying this process that *the body* will be completely cleared. This then causes the unpleasant effects resulting from the Pattern to disappear from the life. This process does not train one to cope with a blockage; it is actually effective in obliterating it.

When the Pattern is a core issue, it deals with extremely high levels of fear because it connects to survival fears. The body has accumulated vast quantities of proof from millennia of past experiences that its "need tos" and "fears of" are eternal truth itself. Removing all past evidence of a Pattern from the body can take time, yet practicing Willingness, Awareness, and Choice not only accelerates this process, it will often bring immediate relief in the moment one uses it.

One must remember that all Patterns are beloved by the ego, which is addicted to their intense emotions and finds an identity within them. In the Warrior experience, the ego exults when it identifies itself as being powerful and it savors the resentment that arises when it can claim to be powerless. The ego uses this resentment to justify attacks against oneself and others. For this reason alone it will attempt to dissuade one from clearing fear Patterns. This is a major reason assistance from the fifth dimension is so important, especially in the initial phases of the clearing process.

One may always choose to clear fear Patterns despite the ego's wishes. Choice does not require one to wait until they feel like doing so; one may choose to remove a Pattern even while experiencing the ego's reluctance to release it. Here is where one can use the Warrior's attributes of courage, determination, and persistence. If one feels the need to "do battle," let it be against the ego and its need to keep the Pattern.

From "The Starborn" Transmission:

We would work with you to clear the body of its historical Patterns keeping you from what you have set out to accomplish. Because we must always honor free will, we ask that you give us your assent during all phases of this clearing process. Through high-level energies, we will rewrite the programming in the DNA from past biological generations. There will also be a period when the body eliminates the chemical cellular memory created by these Patterns. (This is beyond and at other biological levels than the DNA patterning, as well as because of it.)

One might compare this process to clearing out a closet full of outdated objects, representing the body's accumulated "proof" of its no longer valid fear of expressing. For example, every time others criticized you for speaking out, the body recorded and held these experiences as a reminder not to express in the future. All recorded proof of your Pattern must be eliminated from your body and from your life in the weeks and months ahead through application of Willingness, Awareness, and Choice.

Article: "Advanced Willingness"

The longer we apply the Willingness, Awareness, and Choice process, the greater our Soul will demand that we also move forward by taking on more personal responsibility for each of these aspects. In the beginning—as we are merely becoming familiar with our Patterns, learning how to identify them, and exercising basic Willingness by asking the Light Beings to "take this Pattern away"—powerful assistance is afforded each of us by higher dimensions. As we progress, however, our Soul asks us to make changes in our beliefs and behaviors to support the clearing process. We can no longer have the majority of the clearing done passively for us. Merely asking to have the Pattern removed after a certain point will not be as effective as it was in the beginning, because the "training wheels stage" is ended.

There are several ways to misinterpret what Willingness really entails—when one consciously or unconsciously uses their fear Patterns as *an excuse* for their behavior, for example. Saying "I have a starvation Pattern; therefore, I have to eat every hour." or "I always get in trouble for speaking my truth; therefore, I cannot share what I know with others," is not how one clears a Pattern. Using our Pattern as an excuse only reconfirms and solidifies it more firmly in the BodyMind.

Some, who insist they are asking to have the Pattern removed, are really only requesting to have its symptoms eliminated. Sometimes the request is an unconscious one: "Ouch, the Pattern is causing me to feel fear, pain, discomfort, and I don't want these *(but I want to keep the rage.)"* This happens more consciously if the person states, "Take this fear away," believing they have asked to have the Pattern removed. Either case is equivalent to calling in the fire department and asking them to turn off the fire alarm but ignore the fire. Little will change, because the Light Beings will not remove the fear without Willingness to have its cause—the underlying Pattern—removed.

Patterns became stuck in our bodies because we did two things: first, we saw ourselves as "victim" in the Causal Moment, thereby harboring unconscious rage and resentment against our "persecutors." Second, we allowed our egos to become identified with the Pattern: "*I am* abandoned," "*I am* abused," "*I am* unworthy," or "*I am* refugee." Our hidden fear, fostered by the ego, is that if we truly divest ourselves of the Pattern, we will no longer know who we are. Furthermore, we must begin to realize that any form of abandonment, abuse, overwork, or feeling of not belonging has been drawn into our life because our ego holds these to be our true reality. That is how we create our own reality.

Advanced levels of Willingness demand that we take some unprecedented risks: to own responsibility for all that has happened *to us* as being the Universe and those who love us as merely bringing us our Patterns. Release any identity as victim. This must include willingness to release rage and blame against others both past and present. Last, we must disconnect from the Pattern's identity to which the ego is obsessively tied—the "I am" statement.

This leads to the next critical step in the process: the requirements to speak, behave, and think in the new way. If, for example, we carry fearful experiences relating to unjust imprisonment, it can show itself as a powerful aversion to small, windowless rooms. We may even choose our residence and employment based on this reaction. To become completely clear of this Pattern, we must recognize the fear when it presents itself, i.e., at the moment we enter such a space. Next, we must acknowledge our reaction as arising from a Pattern and state that we no longer choose it as our present reality or identify with it. Most importantly, *we must sit down in the room, instead of walking out of it,* as confirmation to our BodyMind that we are beyond allowing the Pattern's emotional reactions to continue ruling our choices and behavior. Whenever these physical and emotional responses arise, they are a sign certain that another opportunity to exercise true Willingness has presented itself.

Another powerful way to look at Patterns is to remind ourselves we cannot fear what we have not already experienced. Having experienced it, we currently hold all of its wisdom in our DNA's library; therefore we do not need to repeat it. If we "own" our prior experiences, recognizing that they contribute to the totality of who and what we are, we honor them. Fearing the loss of all we possess, for example, means we already carry the memory of that particular experience in our body. Acknowledging this fact confirms that. We then can tell our body that it does not need to continually warn us, because we have that "book" in our DNA library and are now wise enough to refer to it if needed, which is not now.

Eventually the Soul will begin to get involved, especially if we neglect to apply the clearing process. If that occurs, when the Pattern comes up again, the emotional reactions may be more intense, in order to prompt real clearing. Those who dally along the Path, ignore the information they are given, or who do not take steps to own personal responsibility for their life will receive what we call "wake-up calls" from their Soul.

Those who work with spiritual energies are held to an even higher standard than those who do not. If they receive various attunements or initiations, with this power comes a commensurate increase in responsibility to clear their Patterns, release all blame, and to align the ego's will with the Higher Will.

From the very beginning we were told that Master Alignment is a Special Dispensation for those diligently working to prepare themselves to take on their Soul Purpose. The only thing preventing them are their outdated fear Patterns. This is why the Soul is particularly interested in our applying ourselves to clearing these from the body. Working on eliminating one's Patterns is a powerful spiritual commitment—and it is an answer to a Soul Call.

Transmission: "Refocusing to the Heart"

This Transmission offers a more biological look at the process of clearing our fear Patterns. Refocusing is actually a more advanced step, still based on Willingness, Awareness, and Choice.

The heart is the center in the body that relates both metaphorically and physically to one's emotional connections. The adrenals are associated with the body's "defend and protect" response, which fosters separation instead of connection. We are referring to both organizing structures within the body—the biological as well as the psychological/spiritual centers referred to as chakras. For example, the body contains an actual biophysical organ known as the heart, as well as a spiritual center called the "heart chakra."

Issues associated with love and emotional relating are biologically and spiritually heart-centered. The focus of the adrenal system is on personal safety and survival. Adrenal secretions further implement the "fight or flight" reaction triggered by the limbic area of the brain. Both the heart and the adrenal metaphorically operate on a continuum; one is more or less able to love and connect as well as more or less mired in fear and anger. The adrenal and heart systems are also closely allied because either one operating in the forefront will have a strong effect on the function of the other. While medicine is aware of this, the deeper implication of their interaction in the individual life needs more fully to be explored.

Modern medicine understands that stress, anger, and fear can lead to heart problems over time; therefore, it attempts to minimize these negative reactions. However, mere preventive efforts are not as effective as those that allow one to refocus from the adrenal's goals to the higher purposes of the heart. Many preventive measures merely attempt to mitigate stress, anger, or fear by masking them, especially when one utilizes mere "coping techniques" to accomplish this. This only creates another form of stress. The body registers such attempts as denying what it believes to be necessary for its survival; hence, it automatically resists these measures. If there is a shift in focus from the objectives of the adrenal system—especially from the need to *be constantly on alert* to protect, defend, and separate—to the goals and objectives of the heart center (connecting and relatedness), the balance in the body moves naturally to a state that is less stressful, despite outer circumstances.

When one operates primarily from the adrenal system, certain hormones are released throughout the body; these act to keep the organism on a state of "high alert." These hormones also diminish other glandular secretions supporting those bodily functions that might drain essential energy should a true attack be imminent. In a similar way, a city gearing up to protect itself from an enemy attack will place all available resources into the hands of its army and put aside those activities not directly connected to its defense. Concerts are cancelled, curfews enforced, while martial law prevails.

Because the adrenal hormones secreted during a crisis are less compatible with total body chemistry, they can cause damage in the body if they continue to dominate beyond their true usefulness. This is like a city remaining on emergency status long after the danger has passed. If it continues to operate primarily on adrenaline, the body will be internally at odds with itself. It will experience added stress resulting from competing demands on its diminishing resources.

The chemical releases governed by the heart are both compatible with and supportive of the entire body's physiology, yet these are the ones "put aside" first when the adrenals are on emergency alert. Over a lifetime in which the body experiences continually high levels of adrenaline, certain glands, such as the thymus, will atrophy from disuse, while others will lose efficacy.

Many people worry about the proliferation of addictive substances and their harmful effects on the body. While they are correct to be so concerned, seldom are they aware that the world's most misused substance is the body's own adrenaline. In moderation, this hormone is a basic component of the body's pharmacology; as generally experienced, however, adrenaline is released over time and in amounts that one may only characterize as addictive. This is as harmful to the body as taking drugs or alcohol in excess. It has a direct effect on heart-lung functions, on the kidneys, liver, brain, the digestive and reproductive systems, and—most powerfully—on the immune system. It hastens the aging process, while all heart-centered operations slow this process down. Adrenaline is the leading *indirect* cause of death, while, ironically, its primary purpose is to promote the body's survival.

As noted, adrenal secretions create an immediate "fight or flight" reaction; in a crisis, this often creates an attempt to separate the conscious awareness from the body as a way to create distance. In a sense, one "leaves their body." Hence, the spiritual/psychological consciousness is immediately at odds with the body awareness whenever one feels threatened. This causes the body to feel even more turmoil, because it truly believes that if consciousness successfully escapes, this will lead to madness or death. Dissociating from one's body awareness tends to worsen the already critical situation. This separation response actually weakens one's ability to handle stress because the total being is out of integrity with itself at the same moment it needs all its resources to prevail.

The body feels threatened by attempts to change its way of operating, especially when those changes might disrupt its survival functions. Yet, if the adrenal system is honored for its proper role in the life and relegated to a position secondary to the heart, the entire body will automatically operate in a less stressful manner. Refocusing one's consciousness from the adrenals to the heart accomplishes this. Through refocusing, one turns their full awareness to the heart's goals and objectives, and the body readjusts into a smooth, calm, energy-efficient way of operating. More is accomplished with less effort and there is a greater sense of personal wholeness and inner enjoyment. One's consciousness and one's body now operate in harmony.

In reality, love is the true basis for all stress reactions. One seeks to protect and defend only what one loves and values. Even the need for self-preservation is a form of love. Unfortunately, humans tend to rely on the adrenal function to guard what is loved, although this goal is more appropriately heart-based. One who is always on alert for danger, making a belief in attack their "prime directive," must also operate at high levels of stress in combination with diminished heart functioning. Operating in this way will cause physiological damage to the heart organ as well as psychological/spiritual damage to the heart chakra. Living more consciously from the heart center, knowing one is safe to connect with others, and infusing Love into all thoughts, words, and actions, will actually provide greater self-protection.

Unfortunately, it is not easy to refocus to the heart while inhabiting a world that functions primarily from the adrenal center. Too many institutions—especially those represented by the media, the military, the business world, sports, and even by the educational system—support an adrenal-based focus. Therefore, individuals working alone and in like-minded groups must make an effort to implement changes. Such efforts will be effective on both the personal and global level to assist in the advancement of all humanity.

Each person who undertakes to refocus from the adrenals to the heart center will experience a positive shift in physical, mental, and emotional health. There will also be noticeable changes within one's life circumstances—since reducing a personal "defense budget" frees one's resources for other uses.

How is refocusing accomplished? With continued Willingness to make the shift in focus; with Awareness in the current moment that Love is the single true goal of all endeavors; and with the consistent Choice of Love and connection over fear in all its forms and manifestations.

To encourage all who desire to refocus from the adrenals to the heart, to live with this thought ever in their consciousness:

> *"I desire to always choose Love in all circumstances.*
> *How then would Love act / respond / believe or perceive*
> *in this situation?"*

Consistently applying the process of refocusing to the heart will eventually set itself in the body as the new, automatic way of being. Reacting first from the heart will become natural, and will replace the instantaneous, adrenal-based attack response. Yet, the ability to protect and defend oneself, if truly needed for the body's safety, will not diminish. What will decrease or will disappear entirely, will be the *automatic need* to live every moment in this manner.

Transmission: "The Expert"

This Transmission, received for a man educated both in Europe and the U.S., includes another powerful technique that is highly effective in changing the life. We call this the "Choose Again" *Process.*

The goal your Higher Self has long sought to achieve is drawing near. This is being able to bring through higher transpersonal knowledge for the betterment of Humanity. We acknowledge your struggles and your seeking, because your Mission was more difficult than you had imagined. Yet, we see how much you have accomplished in this life—a large part of which you yourself are not even aware. It is this lack of awareness that sometimes leads you to feel frustrated and is at the root of your concerns.

You were conditioned to believe that it is important to "keep score." This is a way to know with some level of certainty that one's goals have been attained. You find yourself at a critical juncture in your life, a time when one looks back and attempts to "tally" the score, and you are fearful that in some way you have fallen short—not in material ways, but in those that feed your Soul. Therefore, an explanation is in order; one we hope will give you greater peace.

Before you came into this life, you set certain objectives. To help you achieve these goals, you brought through many fine qualities and characteristics. More importantly, you decided to leave a specific ability behind, and it is this decision that has resulted in difficulties for you. What you chose to reserve was the ability "to know." These two words are more inclusive than you might at first think. While you kept the ability to remember Earth-level knowledge, the "knowing" you chose to bar from your awareness exists at a much higher plane.

You asked not only to remain ignorant of "the Plan" and its objectives; you also wanted to retain little if any awareness of *when* you were fulfilling your goals at the spiritual level. That is, while you might remember physical events in your life, you would not retain their deeper significance or an understanding of their true value in spiritual terms. Normally, it is through recognizing the value of one's achievements that one builds a sense of self-esteem. This has been difficult for you, except as an "academic exercise." While you might be able to list your personal and professional accomplishments, they somehow fail to nourish some deep hunger within you. This is the direct result of restricting your ability "to know." On a practical level, this decision also affected your ability to learn in school, until you finally devised a way to separate academic knowledge from "spiritual knowing."

We wish to examine your decision, to better understand the reasoning behind it. Choosing to block your ability to know was indeed a valid decision when it was made. It is rooted in your desire to advance spiritually, thus removing any impediment to that goal. Prior to this life, after evaluating your growth processes, you determined there were moments when you veered off your spiritual Path and fell into intellectual arrogance. You sought to correct this problem in this lifetime. Yet, the problem itself was merely an unintended result of your wanting to avoid persecution for not knowing enough.

As a Scholar/Teacher, you were sometimes persecuted for what you knew, and at others times for not knowing enough. To escape persecution, you made certain vows, commitments, and sacrifices. Your objective was to acquire sufficient knowledge and stature so that *no one* could ever say you did not know enough on one hand, neither could they block your right to express what you did know on the other. Through strenuous personal effort, you finally achieved a high level of experience in many areas: therefore, you were then considered to be an "Expert." As an Expert you knew that others would not judge you incompetent nor prevent you from communicating what you knew. Being an Expert, however, caused another problem: the tendency to have intellectual arrogance.

Becoming the Expert was a reaction to all that happened to you as a "victim." The victim and the Expert are merely equal and opposite sides of the same Pattern; one lives in a state of feeling powerless while the other exerts "power over" others; however, both are still reactions to fear. The victim represents the "fear of" side of the Pattern while the Expert is your "need to" or "Hero" side. These roles are unintegrated parts of your identity; you alternate between them while also seeking a way to resolve or integrate them.

Because it is part of a fear Pattern, this duality causes you to attract those who criticize your level of knowledge or expression on one hand, as well as those who evoke the Expert's need to prove intellectual superiority on the other. There are times when others perceive the Expert as a "persecutor," because of this arrogance.

Before you incarnated this lifetime, you became very aware of this polarization and its effects. For purposes of Soul development, you made a prelife decision to limit reception of all higher forms of intelligence: visionary thinking, intuitive knowing, and comprehension of universal concepts. You understood from prior painful experience this was the level of "knowing" that would trigger either persecution by others or deep ego pride. To "save your Soul" as well as your body, you decided to restrain your ability to know at these levels. Please remember that you yourself set up this restriction and have lived by this decision.

Now is the time for you to make a new decision—to choose again. You are no longer in danger of being persecuted; neither will you deteriorate into intellectual arrogance. You have used this lifetime well to retrain yourself out of this previous habit. Release yourself from this restriction so that true knowledge and understanding can come through you to serve all humanity. As long as you fear persecution, or that you are capable of harming others through your knowledge, you will continue to live as the ego would have you. By committing all your knowledge, including any higher levels of knowing, to serving humanity, this allows you to fulfill your Soul's objectives.

We have taught repeatedly that no individual can perform their Soul's Purpose work themselves; instead the Soul must be allowed to work "with and through" them to accomplish its ends. You are both a Scholar and a Teacher; therefore, your Soul Purpose work must express itself through your receiving and sharing of information. Willingness to put forward all that you are in Truth, and all that you are capable of doing, and then allowing the Soul to use these aspects to further the Greater Plan, is how one achieves Transpersonal Living.

The knowledge you have acquired within this lifetime is impressive, yet the knowledge you are capable of receiving and transmitting from the higher levels is without limit. When you make a new choice to permit this higher knowing to come through you, accepting that it can neither harm others nor corrupt your spirit, you will be truly free.

How does one "Choose Again"?

- First, by becoming aware of your internal struggle whenever you seem blocked by others. Understand how this also triggers on one hand your need to prove yourself an Expert, while on the other you try to feel "humble" about it. Quite a dilemma sometimes! This recognizes the polarization within you.

- Next, note your frustration when you do not receive all the information you need, a result of your original decision, which also affects other levels of knowing.

- Remember that *you were the only one* who set up this restriction. You are not to judge yourself for having made this decision, because you truly believed it necessary for your spiritual advancement.

- Honor your original prelife decision, your reasons for making it, and its sometimes painful effects throughout your life. This decision has fulfilled its original goal—of this we can assure you.

- Recognize that your decision, while having a valid purpose at the time it was made, is now outdated and no longer needed. Continuing in this manner will actually hamper instead of support your ability to accomplish the Soul's Plan.

- Understanding that everything was a result of the choice that you, and only you, made, means you are *the only one with the power* to reverse this by making a new choice.

- Then choose! Your new decision might be phrased in this manner: "I am now open to receive and to express the full knowledge and understanding of which I am capable where this will serve the highest good of all. I no longer need to limit or restrict my ability to receive higher knowing."

Formerly, you felt unworthy to be an instrument through which transpersonal information could flow. You feared that the greater your knowledge and understanding, the more likely you would become arrogant and egotistical. This will not happen, because—through your experiences in this lifetime—you have achieved the wisdom needed to avoid this trap.

We ask of everyone seeking to advance into Transpersonal Living, "Be willing to give up all to gain ALL." For you this means being willing to give up the restrictions you set up around receiving higher knowing, so that humanity will be better served through your efforts in this direction.

We honor and bless all that you are, and all you have done, and we eagerly await working with you closely in the future.

Part Four:
The Miracle

Introduction

In the beginning, all personal BodyMind Alignment sessions and Transmissions concentrated on the emotional or psychological effects of fear Patterns. Later, we began to receive information on how Patterns impacted us on the physical level and especially how they related to certain medical conditions.

Throughout this book, various Transmissions discuss Patterns together with specific illnesses manifesting in the body. None of this information is meant to replace or counter medical advice; it is intended merely as a new way of looking at the whole situation, a look that—it is hoped—will offer greater insight.

Neither can we assume that the Transmissions point to a single cause for a particular disease; for example, two readings on autism discussed different causal backgrounds for this condition.

This section contains additional insights not only on how Patterns and physical conditions relate, but also on the possibility of significant changes when the Patterns are cleared.

We must remember that there is a difference between healing and curing. Every session offers the opportunity for healing, yet it does not mean that a physical cure automatically follows. We have seen some cases in which this has indeed happened, while in others the client acknowledged that a profound healing had occurred in their life, yet the physical condition was not eliminated.

How can we presume to define the word Miracle? We must approach the following with openness and cautious respect.

Transmission: "The Miracle"

Miracles are simply the natural result of Union with the Divine. They flow out from the One in joint creation. They are outside the bounds of Natural Law, which sometimes protects individuals from their ego follies.

All humans need to learn the effects of their individual choices, and these lessons are recorded in the body. For example, the physical impact of harmful behavior will eventually reflect in the body's health. These effects will grow in intensity if the behavior is repeated. When one begins to notice problems, making new choices may alleviate some symptoms. Despite improvement, some effects will remain in the body to "contain" the information that the behavior is harmful. These effects act as a continuing reminder of the wisdom assimilated in the experience. This is part of Natural Law. It would then take a "miracle" to eliminate these lingering effects from the body. When one moves beyond ego, however, and aligns with the Divine, one also steps outside any limitations imposed by time and the "apparent order of things" and moves into the realm of the Miraculous.

All lessons lead to the discovery of one's Self and to greater awareness of one's connection with the Divine. These lessons are generally hard won, especially in the early stages of Soul growth. The wisdom acquired through the learning experience is recorded in the body—along with whatever physical, mental, or emotional effects were imprinted in the process—to support the future survival of the species.

Before one can undertake most activities, the BodyMind will first scan the DNA's library for any reminders warning of any possibility of danger. If reminders are present, then pain and/or fear will arise in the body to prevent one from going forward. For example, one may lose their voice as a reminder that speaking one's truth can lead to torture or death. Heart problems may connect to past personal or hereditary loss or "heart break." During these experiences, one assimilated lessons about relating, along with any physiological effects on the heart itself—the rapid heartbeat of fear and the weighted sense of grief. Cardiac symptoms might reappear in the present after a severe emotional loss, or even when one merely fears a heartbreak might occur.

Every system within the body contains some record of the effects from past experiential lessons. Some of these lessons use the body as metaphor, while others are more literal. In one instance, a person may have a weak leg because they believe they are incapable of "standing on their own two feet"; while in another, it is a remembrance of a Civil War amputation. Given humanity's vast history, it is natural to expect that there are a variety of physical problems that might arise. While not every illness, injury, or wound will make itself known, there are surely enough to keep modern medicine well employed.

Many of these physical conditions are triggered by the body's automatic survival responses, which process information at a speed faster than today's computers. This speed prevents any delay between outside stimuli perceived dangerous to the physical body and the automatic protective responses. Unfortunately, this hair-trigger ability can operate when the outside stimulus only hints at a former life-threatening event. Today's physical world is less threatening in many ways than in more ancient times, yet in the immediacy of its response, the body acts as if the same level of danger exists. Similarly, the "fight or flight" syndrome is a primitive reaction set up in prehistoric humans, yet it still operates automatically in the modern body.

To move beyond the old BodyMind process of enveloping experiential wisdom within reminders of the pain or fear that birthed it, one must step outside the natural order using *supranatural* means. That which is above (supra) the natural is often seen as miraculous. Within their own sphere, Miracles are the most natural of events, yet when introduced onto this third-dimensional level, ruled by strict cause and effect, Miracles are above the norm and outside it as well.

The Miracle removes the emotional and physical warning signals that surround the body's stored wisdom, encasing it much like the chaff surrounds a kernel of wheat. The Miracle operates at the point of origin, the Causal Moment when the original painful event occurred; hence, it works outside time, while still having effects within it. The Miracle encourages the body, mind, and Soul to retain all the experiential wisdom, while also eliminating the outdated manifestations of emotional and physical pain.

The Miracle cannot occur, however, until the individual cooperates by owning the wisdom. This requires them to take personal responsibility—to recognize that, whatever its origin, *it is their body* holding the Pattern. This is not blame; this is honoring what is true. We have stated time and again: Responsibility means taking ownership of the wisdom earned and learned. The wisdom is sufficient and can stand alone without the emotional and physical container *only if* one accepts that it is the result of hard-earned lessons from their own or their ancestor's experiences. This is the opposite of placing blame on others. In contrast, placing blame leaves the lesson and the wisdom unintegrated. Therefore, recognize that a Pattern is simply wisdom enshrouded by outdated fear, rage, and blame; all of which must be released before its gifts are available.

Any unintegrated lessons—along with their emotional and

physical reminders—actually create one's present circumstances. Whenever a Pattern arises, it is a repetition of a prior situation wherein victim's rage was present. Changing this also allows one to experience the Miracle. Otherwise, attempting to lay blame on self or others means true separation of the "wheat from the chaff" cannot take place.

The Miracle always awaits the instant it can begin its work. As observed and experienced, the Miracle can accomplish its task in but a moment. It is outside time; hence, no time is required for its fulfillment—only willingness. The Miracle arises out of Union, for it cannot occur apart from its Source. Union can only exist when one is sufficiently out of victim mentality. Perfection is not a requirement for The Miracle, only preponderance—there must be more willingness to take responsibility for one's wisdom than need to place blame or judgment on others.

Again, as we have emphasized: Take responsibility, for in responsibility is all power, even the power to perform Miracles.

Transmission "The Spiritual Seeker"

Done for an East Coast business owner, this Transmission helped illuminate how her present physical symptoms were actually the "husk" surrounding the wisdom earned through all her past experiences.

This one is already experiencing a greater Awakening within her consciousness. This is a result of her efforts to clear fear Patterns from the body, as well as a lifelong desire to advance spiritually. As she begins to acknowledge the wisdom she holds from past experiential learning, she also needs to eliminate the physical reminders that "contain" this wisdom. "Containers" are prior illnesses or injuries associated with Patterns to remind a person of the lessons to be assimilated. The infant learns very quickly not to touch a hot stove after experiencing a burned finger. Because of the sensory memory from this single experience, even the infant is self-reminded when warned that an object is hot. The lesson is transferable because the body now associates the word "hot" with the memory of the original burn. The pain felt by the finger is attached to the memory and acts a "container" for this wisdom.

Often, as one strives to bring more Light into their body, and simultaneously becomes more conscious within it, certain minor health issues will begin to arise. The Light has flushed them up to the surface because it wants the person to integrate the wisdom held within the now outdated condition and thereby eliminate further need for the container.

Health issues associated with the intestinal system generally relate to past experiences that engendered the emotion of guilt and the desire for greater discrimination. Guilt held in the body is a powerful reminder to avoid certain behaviors that one decided in the past were harmful to self or others. Guilt triggers certain chemical reactions;

some of these affect the digestive system directly while also affecting other systems more indirectly. These chemical interactions eventually may manifest as an inability of the body to process nutrients, high levels of acidity, improper food digestion, weight problems, and constipation. These are just a few examples of the effects of old guilt remaining in the body from past experiences. In extreme cases, self-judgment will cause the body to attack itself, resulting in immune system deficiencies.

If a negative health condition appears, after identifying the feeling of guilt, it is important to note the situation which triggered it. Next, using discernment, evaluate whether the level of guilt is appropriate under the circumstances. An overreaction occurs if remorse-in-the-moment has engendered guilt far beyond what the situation warrants. Then attempt to discover the hidden lesson. What truth did the body wish to remember? Before integrating the lesson, carefully evaluate whether the information is still valid for the present. It might have been wise, for example, to feel guilt for abandoning a small child in another life to discourage one from repeating this action. Today, however, deciding not to pursue a career because an adult offspring remains at home is an extreme application of this lesson.

Processing the information in this way will allow any physical condition acting as a "container" for the wisdom to drop away. One has brought the lesson and its wisdom into full consciousness. One must also release all forms of self-judgment before any physical conditions can dissipate. If one retains blame for one's prior acts or emotions—feeling guilty for even feeling guilty, for example— then the emotion will remain in the body along with the health conditions associated with it.

Not all prior judgments—those against self or judgments made by others—have a valid basis in reality. Nonetheless, the body may retain strong feelings about what was judged wrong, sinful, or impure in the past. One who survived a disaster in which loved ones died may carry massive amounts of "survivor's guilt," although they were in not responsible. Hence, it is extremely important to be nonjudgmental while assimilating any lessons surrounded by guilt. There may be a valuable kernel of truth that one learned through no fault of one's own, although the guilt would have one believe otherwise. Look then only for the wisdom, acknowledge and integrate it, and allow all else to be released.

As stated earlier, because this one is moving into higher Soul awareness, she desires greater purity. This also prepares her body to receive and integrate more Light. Therefore, any past judgments about being "impure" are now appearing as health problems; these represent a belief in her own imperfection. This is compounded by the fact that throughout history physical illness was often seen as "proof" of being sinful.

It would be well for her to realize these physical and emotional symptoms are not what they may seem. They represent a desire to retain the myriad survival lessons accumulated in the past. Instead of judging herself as less than perfect, it would be best to own the wisdom she has earned and learned from these prior experiences. She is to honor the body's attempts to contain the wisdom using physical and emotional symptoms as reminders. Consciously owning the experience and its wisdom is how we define "taking responsibility," and it is the opposite of self-blame.

Wisdom, standing alone, absorbs and radiates the Light coming into the body, while the emotional or physical container acts to eclipse the Light. Choosing to bring more Light into the world requires one to remove the container that hides the wisdom. In this instance, she is to eliminate the Pattern around a belief that she is impure and thus deserves to feel guilty. Clearing this Pattern will also secondarily assist her in removing any physical conditions resulting from guilt's chemical effects on her body.

Transmission: "The Angel"

This highly inspirational Transmission was received for a landscape developer who was diagnosed with terminal cancer. He is a Light to many who meet or speak to him, especially because of his lack of fear.

It is exceedingly important this one understands who and what he is in truth, as well as why he came into a physical body. This, above all, will assist him now, as well as answer many of his questions. We inform him first that he has seen much in his incarnations on this earth. In fact, we would call him "one-who-observes," for that is his gift, his role, and his identity. He is one who has come into the body yet is not "of" this plane. He is, instead, what we have come to term a "Starborn," which means that he identifies more with his true essence as a being of Light than with his temporary experience in a physical body.

There are many on this earthly material plane now present in the flesh although this experience is alien to them. They have spent most of their existence in those realms in which their body is of a high-vibratory nature as versus a physical one. Those on this earthly plane accept the existence of ones such as these: for he is an Angel. Yes, realize that there *are* Angels who have come onto the Earth to assist mankind in more direct ways. They have done this for several reasons, some of which are unimaginable to humans. This one came to serve by being an observer of the human condition. He agreed to come into a physical body to experience the "trials of the flesh," for without such experience one cannot truly *know*. This is the goal of his existence here, and it serves both realms— that of Heaven and Earth.

Humans, who are also spiritual beings, come to this plane to advance through their experiences on the material level. While they do this, they also lift their eyes and hearts to heaven in supplication when they are in crises or have other difficulties. The Angelic Kingdom has many roles; one is to act as an intermediary between the physical and nonphysical realms. Yet this is difficult if a "message" from one realm cannot be fully understood owing to lack of knowledge on either side. Therefore, occasionally certain beings known as Angels agree to take on physical form to gain the basic knowledge and greater understanding of the human condition. He is one who has done this, for it is his goal to act as a Teacher to those on the other realms after gaining as much earthly experience as possible.

As part of his Mission, he agreed to take on the disease of cancer—a condition that engenders great fear on this plane. That is the purpose of his illness and of all the trauma that it has created in his life; each moment is also part of the lesson he came to learn. Yet there is more: While he is present on Earth and while he lives in a human body, he also is experiencing the gift of free will. This gift does not operate in the same way on the Angelic realm. He came here to observe and better understand how humans use free will—again so he can teach.

Because within his true essence he "knows" how to align his will with the Divine (for the Angels live only to do that), he is learning what it feels like to seemingly act outside the Will of God. For example: It is the Will of the Father that all His children are whole. God does not Will disease, yet He fully allows it to exist if it is chosen for whatever reason (and there are many). In this instance, this one has chosen to experience a powerful, frightening disease for higher purposes, yet it is still a choice that appears to be out of alignment with the Will of God, which is total health.

At his essence level, this is an exciting experience, while at the human physical level it is frightening. We have taught that fear is a sign one is out of alignment with Divine Will; however, because of free will, the Divine allows humans to choose what may also engender fear. Therefore, Divine Will supports his choosing this illness because the Will of God supports human free will at every turn.

In their LightBodies, Angels do not experience death; they can only observe it. Because they have temporal, material forms, humans die. Since Angels cannot "know" death experientially, they see it as a mere separation between the spiritual and the physical bodies. While wanting to be of service to humans who pray not to die, or to prevent their loved ones from death, Angels cannot always understand why life in the body feels so precious to humans. Those Angelic beings who have volunteered to actually experience life and death in the body are as valuable to the Angelic Kingdom as are your astronauts, who risk much to travel into space. They gather information to help their realm and in this way serve all humanity as well.

He has assimilated many other aspects of human life in addition to what it is like to have a serious, potentially fatal disease. He has learned to better understand the everyday trials of living in the body, of having relationships, and even why human beings find it so difficult to see what is true—what might be patently obvious to the Angels seems hidden from humans due to the limitations of physicality. He has earned a veritable "Ph.D. in Humanity" during this earthly experience. Neither is this the first time he has done so. We might even compare his sojourns to "scientific field trips." We also want him to know that, in addition to all he has already accomplished, there is another "assignment" he might consider: accepting the Miracle for himself.

It is never easy for Starborns to take on a physical body. Living in the third-dimensional material form is a trial, one that is often the sum total of a Starborn's Mission, because it is so difficult. Usually, there is such a longing for Home—for their star, their dimension, their realm—that Starborns often spend too much time attempting to leave their bodies. We would make it clear that this is *not* what he has done in taking on this serious illness. It was part of his Mission to do this, and he has fulfilled it well.

If he so chooses, he may now take a different fork in the road. Instead of allowing his condition to lead to separation, he may make a new choice and learn what it feels like to heal the physical form by returning it to wholeness. He is not required to do this, yet he may; neither is he to judge himself if he decides otherwise.

When in distress, humans pray for deliverance, and these prayers lift their physical vibration, which also helps them to advance spiritually. Angels do not need to "suffer" to be moved to prayer, for to pray is part of their very essence. Yet, they also support and encourage humans in their praying. Because of his illness, he has touched and awakened many to pray for him. Those doing this are reaching beyond themselves and also lifting themselves spiritually—another purpose his illness is serving. He has inspired many and continues to do so even at this moment. Should he choose to heal this body, he is then (seemingly) faced with a deep yet unconscious spiritual dilemma: "Am I being too (humanly) selfish by wanting to heal my body, when my illness is serving to uplift others spiritually?"

We wish him to know that there is an another way to uplift others: the Master Jesus did this when he performed miracles by healing the sick and the lame. He healed not only to relieve the one who was sick, he did so to prove the glory of the Divine— and said so! Angels "live" in the Glory of God. Humans, however, must struggle to gain even a small glimpse of this Glory sometime during their lives. Yet every time a Miracle occurs, there is an opening for such a glimpse. Allowing the Miracle would then serve two realms—human and Angelic—because it would be a way to bring the two closer together, for their mutual benefit and for the greater Glory of God.

We ask him to meditate on this, for he has within himself all the power and all the energy needed to bring such healing about; he merely needs to know that he does, and why. This is what we provide for him by telling him who he is in truth, and why he chose to have this experience with cancer. He now has the opportunity to experience something new, something that will also provide a much-needed lesson in Hope.

There is a Path, and it has many crossroads, all of which lead only one place: toward Union with the Divine. There are no choices that are "good" or "bad"; sometimes what looks "bad," such as his illness, has a Divine purpose. Some of the pathways will only make the Journey longer, yet the end is certain, and so the time it takes to complete the Journey—even of one life—is unimportant. He is presently standing at such a crossroads and needs to make his own choice regarding how he will proceed. He cannot make a mistake no matter how he chooses: the "short" way Home or the "longer" one that would call for him to stay in the body for more time. We assure him of this, for either choice is Divine Will and either choice will uplift others around him, albeit in different ways.

He is Loved and greatly honored for merely taking on this difficult Mission. It is already a success, and therefore cannot fail. He has much to teach when he returns Home—whenever that might be.

Part Five:
The Power of Love

Transmission: "The Power of Love"

All creation evolves. While those on this Earth plane might not recognize every "being" or life form existing in the Universe—especially those that are not carbon or silicon based—these are still part of the vast Creation of Father/Mother God.

The Creator is without limit, hence is Creation also limitless in its expression. Within the vastness of Creation, the only common factor is Love, yet definitions of Love—and comprehension of the depth and breadth of its power—are as varied throughout the Universe as the species within it.

Only Love itself can truly comprehend Love. Yet each small organism within Creation is capable of understanding and expressing a small portion of the Power of Love, much in the way one might peer through a single facet of an immense diamond, believing that in so doing one has perceived the whole of its beauty. In the same way, humanity has experienced only a minute portion of the Power of Love during the millions of years of life on this planet.

If asked, each being in conscious existence would define Love as they wish it to be. This includes all of Nature, which also holds a limited comprehension of the Power of Love. To the tree, it is rain and sun and room to grow. To the ocean, it is clouds and wind and countless life forms that give meaning to its existence. To the clouds, wind, and sea creatures, the vast ocean itself is Love. Note in these few examples how various aspects of Creation perceive Love within and through other parts of Creation. That is because all Creation is an expression of Love, all Creation is composed of Love; therefore, every part of Creation manifests the Power of Love to all other elements of Creation. Only human beings have forgotten this and attempt again and again to "find" Love, although it is all around them.

When sought, Love is always found, yet rarely is it recognized for what it truly is. This leads to frustration and endless cycles of ever greater seeking, finding, and nonrecognition of Love. It is these endless cycles of seeking that define the history of this planet: its wars, scientific achievements, art, and tragedies. All are a means of seeking Love, as Love is defined in that time and place. To the King, Love is earthly power. To the Warrior, it is victory. To the Scholar, Love is knowledge. To the Artist, it is the freedom to express. Each is true, yet is each also viewing the Power of Love through a very small facet carved in a universe-sized diamond.

When that which one seeks is not found simply because it is has not been recognized, then frustration turns to fear and anger, which are polar opposites of Love. Yet that which is "opposite" is merely another expression of the same thing. There is only Love, sometimes expressed and known in that form, and sometimes experienced as fear, which is Love "upside down." The form is less important than the content, for found within all expressions of fear is the overpowering belief that that which one Loves is somehow in danger.

There would be peace, abundance, freedom, and even health in a very short time if this truth is grasped: that Love is all there is—or ever was. That both the Seeker and the Sought are Love and that which comes into the life in response to the seeking is also Love. This Truth, if recognized, would stop the endless cycle of frustration. That which one desires is always and only Love. The one who seeks does so because they do not know themselves *to be Love*; hence, they feel driven to find it outside themselves. When they realize they are Love, all need for seeking is over. When they recognize that only Love can come to them because only Love—

in all its wondrous forms and expressions—is all that exists, they will cease their endless searching. All pain and suffering will end, all sense of lack or longing will disappear, and only fulfillment, wholeness, and peace remain.

This is the Power of Love, and it can be realized if one strives to eliminate from the mind and body the ego-generated belief that there could be something—that there could be *anything*—other than Love.

Transmission: "There Is Only Love"

Love that is real must express, and by its expression does it mirror the Divine through outward creation. Father/Mother God Loves, and All-That-Is is an expression of that Love. Nothing exists except the Love of the Divine Expressed.

As the energy of Life, Love is never static; it grows, flowers, and produces fruit that seeds the next level of growth, in a never-ending cycle of expression. Love multiplies itself; all living creation is also gifted with the ability to express Love through its own creation, much as the tree brings forth its flowers and its fruit. Each human thought, feeling, or action is the creative offspring of a Child of God, with the Divine as its ultimate Source.

All humans carry within their DNA a part of the ancestors who fathered their existence; in the same way then does every human expression contain a spark of that which is its Source. God is never apart from Her creation, for God is All-That-Is. That which is apart from the Divine does not exist, neither could it even be conceived of, for in the very moment of its conception it has then come into existence as an expression of the Divine.

In a magnificent outburst of Creative Love, humanity was given the priceless gift of free will. This gift forged an intimate link between the Divine and humanity, allowing human beings to act as co-creators—to extend and express Love and to bring forth Life. While this is easily seen in the creation of a child, co-creation applies to *every* act, thought, and word. *All* are the extension and expression of Love, because they are created through the exercise of free will; to judge them as less is to mock both the gift and the Giver. The First Cause is All-That-Is and the Second Cause is the co-creating human. If all of Life is viewed from this perspective, where, then, is sin? Where, then, is "darkness"? Where is the victim?

All of Nature assists humanity's journey to greater awareness of Love's expression. One can use any aspect of Nature as a metaphor: Genesis notes that the stars in the heavens are given to be "signs and wonders." The vines are another example. Each year the grapes "express" themselves in unique combinations and thereby produce vintage or vinegar. In the same manner do you also express the totality of your efforts, both above and below the surface of your life. You, too, take in the Light, or reject it, absorb wisdom from the "dark soil" of your experiences, or are made rancid with judgment and rage.

As grapes are the extension and expression of the vine, while the wine is the extension and expression of the grape, so are you the extension and expression of the Divine. All that you say, do, and think becomes either "vintage wine" or "victim's whine." Yet understand that even this difference in form matters not, because all—including yourselves—are still seen, known, loved, and accepted as the extension and expression of Love.

God is in the dark and in the Light, in the "good" and in the "bad." To fully grasp this understanding is to also release the need for judgment, to heal the separation, and to return again to the Home one never left, except in their "dream of forgetfulness." Dreams exist in the darkness of the night, and quickly scatter in the growing light of dawn. With the coming of the Light, the Dreamers awaken to remember who and what they are. In awakening from the present darkness the Dreamers will begin to know themselves as the Love of the Divine expressing Itself. Then, in their growing wakefulness, they will begin to see all about them the fruits of their own creation; these fruits are their expressions of The Love That They Are.

When this understanding is embraced in full clarity, the world and all that is in it will be seen in a new Light. Now does Love seek to move its expression into a newer form, into a higher octave of itself. This will be expressed through the Awakening—the coming transformation of the human species.

God is All-That-Is, and all that is, or ever was, is God. Love is the Ground of Being. Love is the Root, the Flower, and the Fruit of the Tree of Life. To exist is to Be Love. And to then express that Love through creating is to be the true and acknowledged Child of the Father/Mother God.

Transmission: "Master Alignment"

The word "alignment" carries several connotations, the first one being equality—that is, one who aligns with another is generally neither subject to them nor their inferior. Both parties within any true alignment are seen as equals, although each may also possess their own unique qualities and characteristics.

The purpose of an alignment is to create synergy—to bring together the attributes of one side with those of the other for the mutual benefit of both. What might seem a weakness or detriment on one side actually may be what is most desirable to the other. It is the merging of all aspects that creates something greater than either one could achieve alone.

Alignment also carries a connotation of harmony, for there is a blending of energies that must occur before any true alignment can take place. There are ease and comfort, at times even a sense of familiarity, within an alignment—as if the piece that was missing has now been found.

Because many are struggling to support themselves and their families—often working under circumstances that do not reflect their true Selves—there is a great hunger for that which feels supportive, honors self-worth, nurtures, enhances personal power, and that which flows in balance. As we use the word, all of these are inherent in the term "alignment."

The ultimate goal of Master Alignment is Union between humanity and the Divine, yet this Union must be preceded by individual, personal integration, and further, by Alignment or Union with one's Higher Self. These are the three levels of Alignment that humanity has been seeking to attain since the first moments of Creation.

It is as if, in moving out from the Creator at the moment of their inception, all beings set forth on a mission to discover and realize themselves; yet it was also the Divine Who perceived and Who *was perceived* within the wonders of Creation. One looked upon the sunset so the Divine could view its magnificence, one inhaled the perfume of the rose so the Divine could breathe in its beauty, one drank full of the gifts of the world so the thirst of the Divine was quenched.

All the while, as one ever continued to seek, all the while, as one grew in the greater knowledge and awareness of Self, did one then find that which they sought: themselves. This is why we have repeatedly taught, "All seeking is seeking for the Self." Yet in seeking the Self were they also seeking God; in attaining the Self, do they also reveal the Divine.

The purpose of all endeavors on this plane can be reduced to this simple understanding: All that is sought, all that is gathered, all that is achieved, is the Self, and in so doing does one also find God. Then may the two again unite, for the journey is complete, the destination reached, the Alignment accomplished, and the partnership enriched by all that was learned, felt, endured, won, lost, and loved. Then shall nothing experienced be seen or judged as failure or "sin," for its place in the Plan will be fully understood and embraced.

Come forward, then, all of you who traveled out from your Father's house so many eons ago, for you now return carrying Treasures of inestimable value in every cell of your Being—it is the Wisdom acquired through all that you have experienced, suffered, and learned. In seeking and attaining yourself have you allowed the Divine to find Himself, and for this His gratitude to you is beyond measure. Welcome Home!

Transmission: "Out of the Silence"

Silence. In the moment before Creation there was Eternal Silence, and the Void. There was nothing to see, hear, feel or comprehend. And then, All-That-Is "breathed" Itself outward—Love expressing Love in ever greater Wholeness and Oneness of Being. Love comprehended Itself in Love and through Love until what was unmanifest but a moment before became manifest in a multiplicity of dimensions, and in many different forms.

Did the One "divide" into the "many"? No, for there has never been nor ever will be separation. To divide is to create space of non-Oneness between segments; yet when the space itself is also an inseparable part of the Oneness, there can never be apartness. There is only the Oneness, and It is Whole and Complete. It is Itself, and nothing else exits outside of It.

Yet, after the Oneness extended Itself, the segments perceived the illusion of separation as well as an "identity" apart from the One. This was a function of their state of awareness, for at the initial levels of consciousness they could not embrace the enormity of the One—nor can they still. To do so would cause an immediate merging back into the Oneness. Yet, what *is* possible is moving into a new and higher level of awareness—an Awakening into greater consciousness.

Before the moment of the new Awakening there is again the Silence, the darkness of the Void, and a state of not knowing how the next level will manifest.

Each day, as human beings awaken from sleep they replicate the moment of Creation. From out of sleep's silence and its darkness springs forth the day in all its wonderment. First, there is an awareness of the body, then the space around it. The awareness continues moving outward to include sensations, feelings, and thoughts of present and past events. What was unmanifest again becomes manifest.

While one sleeps, only a portion of their consciousness is unaware, at much lower levels they still retain some sense of the body's processes, its surroundings, and even its history. In just moments upon awakening, all that was outside of consciousness as one slept is once again called forth into awareness. Sleep deadens only one's physical, waking awareness; yet to one in a deep state of sleep all is seemingly "lost" and can be regained only through awakening.

So is it now. Humanity has been in a deep "sleep" at a certain level of consciousness. While apparently awake and aware of the physical, mental, and emotional aspects of the body, and the cacophony of daily events, humans have still never been *fully conscious*. There is a higher level of awareness that has slumbered on. This level now strives to Awaken—a burgeoning process we call your Greater Birth.

Between one moment and the next, between silence and awareness of sound, between darkness and awareness of light, between emptiness and full comprehension—this is how swift is both the waking from sleep and your Greater Awakening. For but a moment longer there is the Silence, and the Void that precedes the Light. Even now the body stirs in its sleep as the Dawn approaches...as the Silence recedes.

Appendix

Miracle Money Technique

Statement:
"This week I will experience a Miracle having to do with Money."

Rule 1. When the Miracle happens, in some way acknowledge it.
Rule 2. Repeat the statement only when you are in doubt or fear,
AND after Rule 1.

Commentary on the Rules:
Rule 1. This can be tricky—it is actually training in "new vision."
Can you "see" the miracle when it comes? This will be more clear
when you learn about the phrase "having to do with money" below.
One may simply say, "Aha, here is a Miracle having to do with money!"

Rule 2. This statement is not an affirmation that is to be repeated
constantly! Say it, and let it go to work. If, however, you find that
something disturbing occurs to bring in doubt that this will work,
or a fear about money arises, then firmly repeat the statement, and
again let it go. As soon as you have acknowledged a Money Miracle,
repeat the statement this way, "And this week I will experience
another Miracle having to do with money!"

Purpose of the phrases:
"This week": These words accomplish two purposes; the first is
to create a known framework of time in which the Miracle will
occur. Without these words the time is too vague, encouraging
doubts to arise.

The second purpose is to fool the inner "judge" who has no
faith in abundance. This "judge" is of the ego and encourages our
fears around money. However this "judge" tends to be lazy; upon
hearing "this week," it sets up a strategy to send out doubt and
fear messages three or four days after the statement is made. In
actuality the Money Miracle will occur much sooner, thus getting
around the tactics of the "ego-judge."

"I will": This is NOT a future tense verb. It is an expression of personal will phrased in such a way as to again fool the ego. If there is one word in this statement that is to be emphasized it is the word *will!*

"Experience": When one receives and then sees the Miracle, there is a real "aha!" reaction in the body.

"A Miracle": It is critical to have *no expectation* of the source or the amount of the Money Miracle. Do not think, "Now I will get a raise" or "Now I will win the lottery." A penny on the floor can be as much a Miracle having to do with money as an unexpected refund from the IRS for $850! Acknowledge the penny (which appears primarily to let you know that the technique does work, and you need not be in fear) and then repeat the statement per Rule 2.

"Having to do with Money": It is easy to see a Money Miracle when it involves actual currency, and more difficult when you receive something of value that did not require an exchange of "green pieces of paper." Once acclimated to acknowledging unexpected money as a "Miracle," you will find the process may change—you begin to receive things at no cost. (Being taken out to lunch, a set of books, a free ticket to a concert.) This phrase is the one most associated with Rule 1—if it does not directly involve cash, check or money order, are you able to perceive that the Money Miracle has occurred?

Additional Applications

This same technique can be used to experience a Miracle in other areas of your life, as long as you do not try to combine them in the same sentence or do them back-to-back. Give each one time to work.

... I will experience a Miracle having to so with <u>my job.</u>
... I will experience a Miracle having to do with <u>a relationship.</u>
... I will experience a Miracle having to do with <u>time.</u>

Additional Vows

Oaths of Retribution

If, in any lifetime, I or anyone on my behalf, made an oath of vengeance or retribution, I hereby rescind such oaths for now and for all time.

Vows of Commitment

If, in any lifetime, I made vows or promises committing myself to another, I hereby rescind such vows or promises for now and for all time. If, in any lifetime, another made vows or promises committing themselves to me, I hereby release them to Divine Light and Love.

If, in any lifetime, I made vows or promises which now prevent the full expression of my Love to others and my ability to receive Love from others, I hereby rescind such vows and promises for now and for all time.

Vows for the Spiritual Life

If, in any lifetime, out of anger toward the Divine, I vowed to reject the presence of Spirit in my life, I hereby rescind such vows for now and for all time.

"My Work as an Expression of the Love That I AM"

An Artist can be anyone who wants a purpose that stimulates and excites them, a work that so expresses their essence that they revel in it, instead of dreading another day of grinding drudgery. Our Soul Purpose work cannot be found in the want ads, because it does not exist in the same way as other occupations.

The Guides gave us an exercise to help us co-create the work that best expresses the Love that we are. This process is powerful and efficacious. In offering it, the Guides explained:

"You have all asked, 'What is my work? What is it I am to do?' and yet you have been met with resounding silence. The reason is that you are going about this backwards. Understand that your particular Soul work is who you are; no one else can find it for you. Therefore, if you will tell us who you are, and how your work reflects that, we will help you create it."

Directions: Create a form of several pages containing two sentences, one beginning "I AM," the other "Therefore, my work."

Complete the sentence beginning with "I AM" by writing in a personal quality, characteristic, or a heart's desire. Keep it positive instead of putting in something you do NOT like or do NOT do.

Complete the second sentence beginning with "Therefore, my work" by doing your best to indicate how that reflects in your work. Keep this sentence in the present tense (is, has, allows), not the future.

Examples:

I AM *one who likes a lot of variety.*
Therefore, my work *has change of pace, face, and place.*

I AM *intelligent and insightful.*
Therefore, my work *stimulates my mind and has meaning at several different levels.*

I AM *introspective and spiritual.*
Therefore, my work *allows me the opportunity to enhance my personal and spiritual growth.*

I AM *social and like working with people.*
Therefore, my work *allows me to interact with others.*

I AM *independent and resourceful.*
Therefore, my work *gives me autonomy and freedom to make choices.*

Master Alignment Programs

Prerequisites
"The Diamond Body": Introduction to Master Alignment
"Transforming the DNA": Level I Training
"Birthing Homo Spiritus": Level II Training:
Advanced Alignment Intensives

Advanced Training and Certification
Master Alignment Awakener Attunement
Master Alignment Practitioner Classes
Power of Love I: Acceleration
Power of Love II: Healing

Dates and the locations of all programs,
are listed in the Master Alignment Newsletter
Contact us to sponsor a Program in your area

Master Alignment Newsletter
The Newsletter is published 10 times a year.
Subscription is $25/yr U.S. $35/Foreign

Contact Information
email info@masteralignment.org
or write us at
1080 W Patrick St. #188
Frederick MD 21703-3972

Note: At present we do not have a Master Alignment web page.
We anticipate creating one sometime in 2002.

Author

Michelle Andersen, a former attorney, is the originator of Master Alignment. She and her partner, Richard Rylander, live in Maryland. Michelle is currently working on two more books in this series: A second edition, updating and expanding *Awakening to Our Greater Birth* and a new book titled *Homo Spiritus*.